Achieving Performance Results

Boosting Performance in the Virtual Workplace

William S. Hubbartt

i

© 2019, William S. Hubbartt
All Rights Reserved
ISBN-13: 9781699835005

Contents

Introduction

"Congratulations on your assignment as the new Project Team Leader for the ABC Project. You have been selected for this opportunity because of your unique abilities and accomplishments as an SME (Subject Matter Expert). You will be accountable to lead this project from concept to completion, and achieve a successful implementation by the start of the coming fiscal year. The future success of the company rests on the success of this project and the results you achieve."

As the top SME in your field, you had all the answers. You were key in solving the problems and were recognized for your individual achievements. But now, there is a new element, as a Project Team Leader, you will be expected to lead and motivate the project team members. You will now be working with and through other team members to bring the assigned project to completion, on time and on budget.

Whether your new leadership assignment is called Team Leader, Project Leader, Group Leader, Supervisor, or Manager, you will quickly learn that there is a whole new skill-set needed to get results through working with others. These new skills include activities such as planning, scheduling, coordinating, facilitating and motivating team members to do their part to accomplish the team objective.

For many team leaders, the employee relations part of the job presents the greatest challenges. These employee relations activities can range from employee selection, training, motivating and managing the assigned workforce to provide the products or services of the organization. One of the most difficult aspects of this employee relations challenge is referred to as performance management. It involves the management of employee performance to achieve optimum results. Many organizations use some measure of performance to determine how to fairly reward deserving individuals.

These new people issues will create questions such as:

-How can I get better results from my team members?
-What's the secret for dealing with the new generation of workers?
-How can I effectively manage a virtual work team of people I don't even know?
-What is the best way to deal with an employee who just doesn't seem to fit in?
-What is the best way to measure results?
-Management says that it "Pays for Performance," but how can I apply that to my team?
-How can I get rid of a team member who just does not do the job?

Achieving Performance Results is a handy reference guide on the performance management process. This publication has been developed to guide the Team Leader or Supervisor to improve performance results and to better correlate those results to rewards. It provides useful tips, ideas, and checklists to promote improved performance, help address performance problems, assure more meaningful performance discussions, and to better correlate performance and pay.

The Appendix contains a self-audit checklist, sample policy, performance rating definitions, and work-sheet to guide pay-performance discussions.

There are many kinds of performance management systems with various policies, procedures, and formats. This manual is designed to complement those systems by providing sound advice for the Team Leader or Supervisor by providing tips on dealing with common aspects of defining goals, discussing job performance and rewards with employees.

William S. Hubbartt
November 2019

The Evolving Workplace

The Irony of Change is that it is Constant.

We see this in our lives and we see it in the workplace. Our fore-fathers coped with change, just as we do today.

In years gone by when our country began, Americans lived in an agrarian society. While some individuals fished and others hunted, most individuals and families supporting themselves by tilling the land, working as farmers. Some individuals developed specials skills and crafts providing their services to others. The craft-oriented society evolved to larger scales resulting in the emergence of manufacturing of goods, tools, and weapons. Manufacturing evolved further when creative individuals created machines capable of mass production and providing transportation that exceeded the capabilities of horse and animal-powered transportation. Electricity was harnessed for lighting and communication. We took to the air and revolutionized travel with planes, trains, and automobiles. Mechanical tabulators evolved into programmable controllers and then to computers.

The irony of change is that it is constant, and constantly accelerating.

Now, smartphones put powers into our hands that were unimaginable a generation or two ago. We are moving from the digital information age to what has been referred to as the fourth industrial revolution. Prime examples include artificial intelligence now being used to facilitate decisions while automobiles are being programmed to be self-driving and factories once filled with workers on production lines now hum with the efficient programmed movements of robotic assembly, welding and painting devices.

Many individuals embrace new technologies and the changes they bring to daily lives and to the workplace. And yet, any manager who has ever introduced change into a workplace has encountered resistance from employees who prefer doing things the old way, "the way we've always done it before." But, time marches on, and change happens. Organizations, like living creatures, adapt and survive, or die.

Organizations operate to provide a product, an object or device that others find useful and want to acquire, or a service performing some activity that others want or need. Organizations in the private sector, sell their product or service and seek to make a profit in order to continue in business. Not-for-profit entities may provide a product or service at some cost while not seeking to make a profit, and the government provides certain services such as education, protection, public safety, or infrastructure development and maintenance paid for through taxes.

In all of these organizations, there remains one common element: people. While many work processes have or are becoming more automated, the individual employee remains an important part of the process, and those who lead or manage, individuals themselves, must interact with other people to obtain results.

There remains one common element: people

This thumbnail overview of workplace change brings us to note many of the current changes impacting upon the evolving workplace. Cited in no particular order, here are some of the significant new changes in the workplace that affect how managers manage and employees perform in the workplace.

The Digital Generation – In an article entitled "The Digital Generation," author Nickey Hockley cites one description which characterizes Digital Natives as those who have grown up using technology and the internet, as distinguished from Digital Immigrants who have come to technology later in life. The Digital Native performs tasks entirely from the screen while the Digital Immigrant is more likely to access information from the screen and then print out and work from paper copies of data. In another characterization, Hockley cites the term Digital Resident, a person who lives a significant percentage of his or her life online through social media and portrays self-image through online networks, distinguished from the Digital Visitor who uses the web as a tool but is unlikely to fully expose their identity online.[1]

Telecommuting – Many firms now allow a wider variety of flexible workplace alternatives, permitting employees to perform work tasks at home or from alternative work sites. Often referred to as telecommuting or telework, such practices permit employees to perform work tasks from home on an ad hoc or part-time or full- time basis. Such practices are particularly adaptable for knowledge workers, or for workers whose job requires data access, or entry to an employer computer system using desk-top or portable lap-top computers or tablets.

Virtual Work Teams – The information age has connected individuals through the internet via smartphones, tablets, laptop and desktop computers allowing many individuals to perform work tasks away from the central office or factory that was once the primary place of work and employment. The interconnectivity of devices allows individuals to work in the office or plant, or at home, or while traveling. Software and systems now allow instant communication in mediums that may be visual, verbal, and/or electronic messaging or e-mail. Documents, and data and graphic images can be created, shared, viewed, edited, circulated and stored for instant retrieval and use. Work team members may be across town, in another city, or in another country. Further, the virtual work team members may be employed by the employer or they may be an independent contractor or another contingent worker as described below.

The Gig Economy – This term has been applied to describe a growing number of individuals who have elected to engage in self-employment, obtaining work on a project or job by job basis. Such individuals often find independent contractor employment opportunities through web sites or cell phone apps that offer to connect self-employed workers with employers who are seeking individuals with their particular skills. One example of this business model is the ride-sharing services – a form of non-regulated taxi service - offered through organizations like Uber and Lyft. Their drivers are independent contractors who set their own schedules, accept or reject offered assignments and make all contacts and arrangements for services with customers through the ridesharing app.

Contingent Workforce – Other examples of contingent workforce arrangements include temporary help work agencies and employment agencies that provide contract workers with specified professional skills or credentials for specified or short-term assignments. Individuals in this category of employment are actually employed by the employment agency and paid by that agency while performing tasks at the client employer's job site or work from home basis.

New Employment Relationships – Another example of an emerging employment relationship is referred to as employee leasing, where a Professional Employer Organization (PEO) offers to handle all employee management tasks and responsibilities for an employer by hiring and providing payroll, payroll taxes, and benefits for all the employees of the business in return for agreed fees for these services. The effect of these varied employment relationships can create what is referred to as a dual employment relationship where two or more entities are involved in directing and or supervising and or paying employees to perform specified jobs. These issues become significant when there is a workplace injury or workplace decision or incident that might be considered to be employment discrimination.

Changing Employment Roles – The traditional employer-employee relationship is altered by one or more of the work arrangements described above. In the traditional employer relationship, the manager could hire and fire the employee and the employee could seek and accept and quit employment at will. These are elements of what may be referred to as employment at will, a legal term defining the employment relationship. Employment at will prerogatives may be altered by certain state or local or federal statutes, and by court decisions interpreting the law. The laws define what constitutes a supervisor or manager, and certain laws may affect employees differently than supervisors. A person who functions as a project leader or a team leader may, or may not be a supervisor under the interpretations of the various laws. While this explanation may seem muddy and unclear, one reason is that it is a matter that is in a state of flux.

Employment laws from the 1930s to current years are now being applied to new workplace arrangements that were not anticipated when the laws were originally passed by state legislatures or by Congress.

Performance Appraisal Under Fire – The annual performance appraisal remains a standard tool in the human resources management toolbox of an overwhelming number of employers according to survey data (reported later herein). But this annual ritual has come under fire in recent years as growing numbers of high-profile firms are opting for alternative means to manage employee performance. Supervisors lament the struggle to complete the annual performance appraisal exercise while employees complain that the process is an unfair torment. Management wants to recognize and reward top performers while human resources staff endeavor to implement suitable solutions.

Summary

The workplace is changing, but the common element is people, working together to accomplish results. The ideas and suggestions covered here are intended to help team leaders to effectively interact with other people to obtain improved performance results.

Working Together

Serving Clients and Customers

Every entity exists for a specific purpose. Privately held and family-run businesses seek to create their niche in the marketplace by providing a particular product or service. The larger corporations and publicly owned entities compete in the national and international marketplace to provide products and services that fulfill the needs of their clients and customers. Not for profit entities render specific services tailored to the needs of the consumers seeking their unique specialized assistance, while various public sector governmental units render services specified by constitution or legislated by the law or regulation.

As the entity grows, it hires employees. These employees then, are expected to carry out the assigned tasks of the entity. The owner or manager of the entity determines what work is to be done, and defines a job or jobs to perform the tasks. As the entity grows, more employees are added. Soon, certain individuals are designated as team leaders or supervisors and managers. The team leader is part of the employee group, responsible to give direction and instructions to members of the group while performing his or her own tasks that are part of the group's work.

The workgroup leader must endeavor to achieve goals, and seek ways to improve performance results

For an entity to get the most effective result from employees, it is recommended that management identify its mission and goals. The challenge to leaders of the entity is to align employee tasks and performance with the entity's goals.

Leadership Role

As a team leader or supervisor, it is your job to achieve results that further the goals of the organization by leading and motivating your workgroup. Not only must the workgroup leader endeavor to achieve organizational goals, but you must also continually seek ways to improve performance results. For some new or inexperienced team leaders, this task may be seen as an uncomfortable activity to be avoided. Yet, to be successful as a team leader, learning to effectively handle performance management accountabilities can significantly contribute to your success as a team leader.

As detailed in the congratulations letter shown in the introduction of this book, the new group leader -whatever their title: team leader or supervisor or manager – assumes a new responsibility, that of directing the work activity of other individuals. This activity requires more than just the technical knowledge or skill relating to the job activity, it also requires the group leader to deal with the employee relations aspect of running their workgroup. The group leader is responsible for their own work and the work of others in the workgroup. It is a whole different skill set that includes planning, communicating, directing others, coordinating, training, motivating, reviewing results and taking corrective action to prevent or resolve problems that may arise. In two words, the new job element for the group leader is People Skills.

In many organizations, human resources specialists create systems and procedures to help the organization to effectively deal with people issues to achieve defined goals. These processes are often referred to as performance management. Performance management processes designed to aid team leaders and supervisors to motivate subordinates, manage employee performance, deal with performance problems, and reward results.

Survey Findings

A large majority of employers use performance management processes to improve employee performance. Often such processes are correlated to employee compensation. Such were the findings reported in a 2017 Inventory of Total Rewards & Practices survey conducted by World at Work with underwriting support from Korn Ferry Hay Group. The survey gathered data about the use of total rewards programs in US companies. World at Work is a leading non-profit professional association in compensation and total rewards.

According to the study, 91% or reporting firms use formal performance appraisals/reviews for some or all of their employees. The study included employers in the private sector-both publicly and privately owned, the not for profit sector and the public sector. When asked whether the entity used formal performance ratings, 80% replied yes, while 16% reported using informal performance ratings.[2]

There are wide variations in the frequency of such practices based on organizational size. For example, 84% of smaller firms, those with fewer than 500 employees, reported use of formal performance appraisals/ reviews, compared to the larger firms whose reported use ranged from 93% to 98% according to survey data. The smaller firms, on the other hand, were more likely to use an informal performance rating process, reported at 21%, compared to the larger firms which used informal processes in the 12% to 17% range, depending on the size of the firm.[3]

While the above data reveals that the use of performance management is fairly common, many human resources specialists concede that there is always room for improvement in the design or use of those systems. For example, in an article appearing at SHRM.Org., researcher Shonna Waters poses the question Should Organizations Pay for Performance? Waters' report suggests that the link between pay and performance might not be as strong as you think, identifying reasons why some firms are taking a look at traditional performance appraisal processes and some are scrapping the old ways. The reason, says Waters is that measuring performance in the new knowledge-based jobs is more difficult compared to measuring performance in sales jobs or manufacturing tasks where the quantity of production is a key performance measure. If the links between performance and rewards are unclear, then performance-based pay plans become difficult to administer fairly.[4]

Data from the World at Work survey bears this out when comparing employer responses in 2017 to the prior year 2016 data. The number of responding employers who reported using formal performance appraisals dropped by three percent from ninety-four percent (94%) and the number reporting use of formal performance ratings dropped by five percent from the prior report of eighty-five percent (85%).[5]

According to Stuart Hearn of Clear Review reporting in a performance management blog, organizations are developing a new performance management culture and minimizing form filling and bureaucracy seeking to simplify performance management processes.[6]

CEB, a best practice insight and technology company recently acquired by Gartner, reported on this trend recently stating that Peter Cappelli, a director of Wharton's Center for Human Resources, has taken a wait-and-see attitude about whether employers will really create a different kind of relationship with employees relating to performance measurement. "For a lot of companies that are thinking about this change, they are just copying what other companies are doing," he says. "We will see a lot of false starts on this thing, and then they will discover their relationship with employees is worse off. The thing I would watch is to what extent this is an ideological battle. Is it all about the money, all about rewarding people? It's an ideological divide that has to do with human nature. And to some extent, that's at the heart of this whole issue."[7]

Summary

Clearly, employers are looking for what works in managing employee performance. Many supervisors candidly acknowledge that their reluctance to address employee performance issues is due in part to a lack of confidence in how to respond to tough questions from employees. *Achieving Performance Results* provides the tools, tips, and techniques to guide the team leader or supervisor step by step through the performance management process, recognizing that employers have a variety of performance management procedures.

New Trends in Performance Management

The Fourth Industrial Revolution

We are hurtling forward in what has been referred to as the fourth industrial revolution. Artificial intelligence (AI) makes decisions, automobiles are safety programmed and soon will be self-driving, biotechnology applies technology to living organisms while manufacturing plants now hum with the efficient programmed movements of robotic assembly, welding and painting devices. These developments are already substantially changing the workplace. Deloitte's 2019 global human capital trends report suggests that businesses must re-invent their ability to learn. One way is for the organization to adapt itself to become a social enterprise. A social enterprise is an organization whose mission combines revenue growth and profit-making with the need to respect and support its environment and stakeholder network.[8]

Deloitte proposes five human principals for the social enterprise, identifying benchmarks for reinvention. These are identified as:

1) Purpose and meaning – giving individuals and organizations a sense of purpose beyond profit to the focus of doing good things;

2) Ethics and fairness – using data, technology, and systems in a fair and trusted way;

3) Growth and passion – designing jobs and organizational mission to nurture passion and a sense of personal growth;

4) Collaboration – building and developing teams and personal relationships;

5) Transparency – operating the enterprise in a way that shares information openly while managing with a growth mindset.[9]

Performance Appraisal Re-examined

According to survey data cited earlier in this book, the performance appraisal remains a commonly used practice by many employers. But this annual ritual has come under scrutiny in recent years as some firms are re-examining ways to manage employee performance. An article from the Washington Post in 2015 reported that, though many major companies haven't yet dropped the practice of performance appraisals, significant numbers acknowledge that their current appraisal systems are flawed. The article cited that 95 percent of managers are dissatisfied with the way their companies conduct performance reviews, and nearly 90 percent of HR leaders say the process doesn't even yield accurate information.[10]

The article went on to report that consulting firm Accenture planned to get rid of performance review and rankings, substituting the process for a more fluid system where employees receive timely feedback from managers on an ongoing basis following assignments. Other readily recognized firms that reportedly abandoned the traditional performance appraisal process included accounting giant Deloitte, Microsoft, Adobe, and Gap. Eager to support a management that wants to recognize and reward top performers while being responsive to employee concerns, human resources staff at a growing number of companies are exploring various performance management alternatives.

Different Strokes for Different Folks

ETS, a British consultancy specializing in employee surveys, leadership development, and HR technology reports in its blog how leading firms have been addressing performance concerns by replacing performance ratings. The consultancy identified the following examples:

\+ Accenture scrapped their ratings several years ago replacing the process with a "more fluid system," where employees receive timely feedback.

\+ Adobe discarded performance management forms and questionnaires with a formal rating or ranking system, and now operates using a continuous process of feedback and improvement referred to as a "Check-in" which isn't documented or recorded.

+ Amazon, a firm that has a reputation of being a high performance-high challenge organization, holds weekly or monthly business reviews where each employee is accountable for an array of metrics.

+ Deloitte has focused on simplifying its performance management process where managers answer four future-focused statements about every team member at the end of each project. The statements assess the individual on issues related to compensation, retention, low performance, and promotion potential.

+ Google abolished its numerical performance rating system in 2014 and replaced it with a peer review system conducted semi-annually.

+ Netflix uses a process of yearly 360 reviews where everyone in the company can provide feedback on co-workers, managers and subordinates, and includes a retention question element.[11]

The Society of Human Resources Management (SHRM) a leading professional association for human resources professionals, offered ideas from its 2017 annual conference in an June 2017 article entitled "How to make Ratingless Performance Management Systems Work," Presenters suggested that HR personnel *create a culture of feedback* approaching performance discussions in more frequent less formal discussions rather than waiting for a formal discussion at year-end. Another suggestion was to *be specific* by identifying specific tasks or deliverables that can be measured. Use structured interviews to *evaluate* the employee and to keep underperforming employees from job-hopping around the organization. Make feedback fun by recognizing the completion of micro-learning activities or having competitions among workgroups. SHRM presenters also suggested that HR personnel should listen *to manager's war stories* to undercover myths about correcting poor performance.[12]

HR Technology Offers Alternatives

As technological changes have affected business operations, so too has the variety of choices offered by applications-oriented software development providers. While a detailed analysis of performance management software and providers is beyond the scope of this publication, many of these vendors do offer valuable information relating to the current trends in performance management. Some selected highlights are summarized here are presented for information only and not to be construed as any form of endorsement or preference of one organization or software package over another:

15Five, a performance management software vendor in a blog by David Mizne, proposes that the following are performance management trends to watch in 2019.

1) Developing employee trust in achieving improved employee productivity will be an important management tool in the coming year.

2) Continuous performance management is the new direction replacing older unworkable performance management processes.

3) Progressive firms are shifting their focus to improving the employee experience. This is a management philosophy that considers an individual's thoughts, feelings, and emotions and being responsive to these elements to maintain quality employee relations and communications.

4) People Analytics will become essential. As companies collect more and better data on turnover, team interaction, employee feedback, providing better data for employment and operational decisions.

5) Focus on Individualized Employee Support will increase. Key examples of this element are the greater use of work teams and remote employment work-sites, and flexible individualized resources to meet the needs of a diverse workforce.

6) Employee Learning and Development will increase and become streamlined to meet the needs of employees and the entity alike. 15Five identifies that 87% of millennials weigh access to professional development and career growth as an important factor in a job.

7) Rethinking job roles will be one way that allows employees to do what they do best. One way entities can achieve this is to adapt the job to the employee's strengths, a process called "Job Crafting."[13]

Clear Review, a British performance management software development and consulting firm, identifies the following performance management trends facing business managers: Stuart Hearn, writing in a Clear Review blog asserts that: 1)

Employee wellbeing will become part of performance discussions, 2) Employee feedback will need to be supported by regular coaching conversations, 3) Performance management will become more meaningful and human, 4) Performance management will focus on how to improve the effectiveness of employees and managers. 5) Artificial Intelligence (AI) will make its way into recruitment, learning and into the performance management process.[14]

Performance Check-ins

A review of performance management trends from numerous sources emphasizes a simpler process with more frequent performance check-ins to replace the prior pattern of a form oriented annual performance appraisal. The trend is towards a more informal performance talk providing feedback to the employee at the end of a task or project, or at a shorter interval that may vary from weekly, to monthly, to quarterly. The nature of the employment and the needs of the job will influence what may be deemed a suitable check-in period. Priorities may be communicated. Goals may be agile and individualized. Performance data or goals or measures or other metrics may be part of the discussion, along with feedback on performance behavior and cooperation with team members. Frequent conversations provide immediate feedback and reaction in response to any identified needs for support or material or supplies. Conversation on the achievement of near-term goals provides a greater opportunity for more immediate recognition providing greater opportunity for motivation. The employee's personal and career development goals are often part of these discussions, and management has an opportunity to put direction to learning or work assignments in a way that supports an employee's goals.

Managing Millennials

Millennials are generally described as individuals born in the 1980s and 1990s. Also referred to as Generation Y, these individuals entered the workforce in the late 1990s and early 2000s and are now in their twenties and thirties. These are individuals who grew up and were schooled in an era when computer technology entered nearly every home and school and workplace. And now, the next generation, sometimes referred to in the media as Generation Z, those born in the late 1990s and early 2000s, are completing schooling and entering the workforce as digital natives. These are individuals who live and breathe and communicate in social medial and the internet using portable technology such as smartphones, tablets, and laptops. These individuals bring new perspectives to the workplace.

Millennials, the largest segment of the workforce, grew up in an era of smart phones, tablets, and laptops. Millennials embrace electronic literacy in their lives and on the job.

Susan Heathfield, an organizational development and HR consultant, writing in The Balance Careers website, offers tips for managing millennials. Heathfield says that there are measurable differences in how millennials were raised and educated and that managers who understand these differences can be more effective when managing millennials in the workforce. Heathfield proposes:

Build a teamwork culture. Millennials participated in many group projects and school activities using teamwork to accomplish tasks. They are familiar with team and group processes; employers organizing staff activities using group and team processes can maximize the skills of the younger workforce in this fashion.

Take advantage of their electronic literacy. As individuals who grew up using technology, its nuances are second nature to them and they can readily aid as entities adopt greater technology in business operations.

Embrace diversity and flexibility. Many millennials identify as multi-racial comfortable with diversity, and they seek flexibility in work activities. Millennials will seek employment with firms offering such flexibility and will avoid or leave rigid employers stuck in old ways.

Focus on results. Firms that focus on structure and processes – things like fixed work schedules and dress codes – will not seem attractive to millennials who prefer to focus on results rather than rules.

Allow telecommuting and remote work opportunities. These are work processes that embrace technology and allow greater flexibility, work environment features that are embraced by millennials.[15]

Guido Stein, a Professor of Managing People in Organizations at IESE Business School of the University of Navarra (Spain) writing in Forbes proposes a number of guidelines that will help organizations to effectively utilize the talents of millennials.

Provide learning opportunities. Younger employees, especially those born in the nineties, have grown up in a culture of immediacy, surrounded by stimuli and eager for new experiences. Managers who can identify opportunities for new skills and assignments for employees who are accustomed to video game "level up" achievement measures.

Balance personal and professional demands. Millennials look for flexibility and autonomy focusing on results and don't want to be tied to an eight-hour office schedule.

Flexible compensation. This group generally values the attractiveness of the work itself and mobility of work and assignments in a relaxed atmosphere. The ability to customize compensation with things like days off, flexible hours, telecommuting and discounts are valued.

Career movement. Millennials are advancement and career-oriented, but not likely to wait indefinitely to achieve their goals. Managers who engage in frequent career conversations with subordinates will have opportunities to tailor assignments that provide diverse experiences and growth opportunities.

Be a mentor. Millennials infamously lack respect for traditional authority structures with rigid protocols. A manager who takes a mentoring approach rather than flexing authority will have greater success in motivating subordinates.

Strong company culture. Millennial employees will be attracted to an employer that displays the culture and values that are in line with their own ideas and lifestyle. The absence of this element will likely contribute to the millennial seeking other employment.

Recognize achievements. Individuals who live and share their activities and accomplishments on social media clearly seek recognition for their achievements. Managers of these employees will need to find ways to recognize performance results.

Recognize the social media lifestyle and find ways to incorporate this characteristic into the workplace culture and activities.

Digital natives need to feel connected. Stein reports that over fifty percent of digital natives say they would turn down a job that denied them access to social networks. Businesses will need to find ways to balance the use of social media with work priorities and work goals.[16]

New Employment Relationships

The Gig Economy

Team leaders and supervisors now find themselves dealing with a variety of employees who may or may not be actual employees of the employing entity. There are many new employment relationships appearing in the workplace. An understanding of these complex issues relating to employment relationships will be important if a team leader or supervisor is to effectively motivate and manage the performance of team members. These new employment relationships have been referred to as the gig economy.

The gig economy is a recent buzz word term applied to describe a growing number of individuals who have elected to engage in self-employment, obtaining work on a project or job by job basis. These individuals are looking for jobs that offer flexibility to fit work around the demands of other life activities such as school, care of children or other family members, or as supplemental or secondary employment. "Flexible jobs give workers choices," was the title of a recent article in the Monthly Labor Review (MLR). The monthly journal published by the U.S. Department of Labor provides data and articles about current events in the American labor market.[17]

New employment alternatives offer greater flexibility for workers.

According to the MLR author Maureen Soyars Hicks, recent innovations in technology and fundamental changes in the economy have led to a decline in the traditional employer-employee relationship and resulted in an increase in the numbers of employees finding work as temporary workers or independent contractors. The article cites data reporting that the number of U.S. workers participating in flexible contract work as their primary job has grown fifty – six percent over the past ten years. The article cited as an example, the digital ride-sharing service Uber, where self-employed individuals use their own car to provide rides for a fee to customers seeking on-call transportation. The Uber drivers are classified as independent contractors who log onto the Uber ride-sharing phone app to receive ride requests, and to accept or decline ride requests, electing to work where and when they choose.

Crowdsourcing

Another recent emerging example of the effect of the gig economy is referred to as crowdsourcing. It is a concept that is based on the wisdom of the crowd. According to crowdworker.com, a website serving as a portal for crowd workers and employers seeking to use crowd-workers to accomplish specified tasks, crowdsourcing is an accepted way to reach economical goals. The most famous example of crowdsourcing is Wikipedia. The platform is fed by the work of writers and editors who collect, update, and care for the articles that are available on the knowledge platform.

The principle is easy: More minds know more than a single one. So, a mass of people combines their wisdom and experience to boost a project. It doesn't matter if you are an individual, a public institution, a non-profit organization, or a company – everyone can benefit from the crowd. The term crowd-sourcing was first used in 2006 by editors Jeff Howe and Mark Robinson when writing an article for Wired Magazine.[18]

There are various crowd working platforms where employers can search for crowd workers, and workers seeking part-time or occasional project work can register their expertise and may be recruited to participate or input into a crowd-working project.

Contingent and Alternative Employment

In addition to its regular monthly data reports, the U.S. Labor Department now conducts periodical studies of contingent and alternative employment arrangements. In a June 2018 press release, citing data drawn from its Current Population Survey, the Department reported that in May 2017, 5.9 million persons or 3.8 percent of workers, held contingent jobs. The Department defines contingent workers as persons who do not expect their jobs to last or who report that their jobs are temporary.[19]

In addition to contingent workers, the survey also identified the numbers of workers in various alternative work arrangements. In May 2017, there were 10.6 million independent contractor workers (6.9 percent of total employment) 2.6 million on-call workers (1.7 percent of total employment), 1.4 million temporary help workers (0.9 percent of total employment) and 933,000 workers provided by contract firms (0.6 percent of total employment). The tabulated data measures an individual's main or sole job, and where an individual may have more than one job, the count includes the job with the most hours.[20]

The Labor Department defines the foregoing job categories as summarized below:

Contingent workers are those who do not have an implicit or explicit contract for ongoing employment. Persons who do not expect to continue in their jobs for personal reasons such as retirement or returning to school are not considered contingent workers, provided that they would have the option of continuing in the job were it not for these personal reasons. These individuals would be employees of the employer, with their salary or wages subject to employment and payroll taxes.

Independent contractors are workers, freelance workers or independent consultants who may be self-employed or may be employed by an entity that supplies independent contractor workers to client firms. Self-employed individuals are not considered to be employees of the employing entity, not subject to payroll taxes, and do not receive protection of labor or employment laws that provide protections for employees.

On-call workers are workers who are called to work only as needed. They may be scheduled to work for a day or several days or weeks in a row. On-call workers may be employed by the employing entity subject to payroll taxes or may be employed by another entity that supplies on-call workers or may be treated by the employing entity as an independent contractor.

Temporary help agency workers are employees assigned to work at the employing entity referred by a temporary help agency who provides their services under a contract. They typically turn in a time slip or other electronically signed certification for signature by the job site employing entity to document work hours, but these individuals are actually employees of and paid by the temporary help agency. These individuals are often workers performing office administrative tasks, or jobs in a warehouse of manufacturing tasks in a factory.

Workers provided by contract firms are employees assigned to work at the employing entity referred by a contract worker agency who provides their services under a contract. They typically turn in a time slip or other electronically signed certification for signature by the job site employing entity to document work hours, but these individuals are actually employees of and paid by the contract worker help agency. These individuals are often workers performing specialized service or professional or executive work.[21]

Pay and Benefits for Contingent Workforce

It is highly likely that the pay and benefits of contingent workers may vary from the pay and benefits package provided by the employing entity for its regular salaried or hourly employees. The U.S Labor Department press release cited above detailed that contingent workers earned less than their non-contingent counterparts, typically receiving approximately 77 percent of the pay of regular full-time employees. There are many factors that may influence pay rates, including differences in the jobs held by the workers, their demographics, and the pay rates provided by the actual employing entity who contracts with the employer to refer temporary workers for job assignments.[22]

Likewise, benefits such as employer-provided health insurance provided to full-time employees were likely provided only half the time to contingent workers. Contingent workers employed and paid by a temporary help agency or other employment contracting service may or may not be provided such benefits, depending on the practice of the employment service employer. Such contingent employees may seek health insurance coverage from a spouse or family member or may elect to pay for individual coverage. The same holds true for employer pension and retirement plans.

Individuals who are self-employed independent contractors or freelancers are considered to be in business for themselves and are therefore accountable offer their services at a competitive pay rate in order to obtain employment. Independent contractors are responsible to cover their own payroll taxes and insurance or retirement benefits if any.

The difference in pay and benefits has been described as one of the down-sides of the gig economy. Independent contractors and freelancers do not receive protections of various labor laws designed to protect employees, such as unemployment insurance, workers' compensation insurance, and anti-discrimination complaint resolution. Because the independent contractors are not employees of the employing entity, they are not eligible for equal pay law protection, coverage of health insurances or retirement plan participation.

Projected Growth of Alternative Work Arrangements

As shown above, the use of alternative work arrangements has grown substantially over the past ten years. This trend will continue according to survey data published in the Deloitte Global Human Capital Trends Survey of 2018. The portion of firms responding to the Deloitte survey reporting that their use of alternative work arrangements will remain the same or grow in the next two years is shown below:[23]

Labor category	Percent planning same or greater use
Contractors	83
Freelancers	85
Gig workers	84
Crowd workers	83

Employee Leasing Relationships

Another example of an emerging employment relationship is referred to as employee leasing, where a Professional Employer Organization (PEO) offers to handle all employee management tasks and responsibilities for an employer by hiring and providing payroll, payroll taxes, and benefits for all the employees of the business in return for agreed fees for these services. The effect of these varied employment relationships can create what is referred to as a dual employment relationship where two or more entities are involved in directing and or supervising and or paying employees to perform specified jobs. These issues become significant when there is a workplace injury or workplace decision or incident that might be considered to be employment discrimination.

Summary

One of the fastest-growing segments of the workforce in the new millennium is the number of employees involved in contingent and alternative work arrangements. Many of these are short term and part-time work assignments or workers in jobs with temporary or contract employers that refer workers to job assignments. These new employment alternatives offer greater flexibility and scheduling opportunities for workers who may have other commitments relating to family, schooling, or those seeking to supplement other full-time employment. Team leaders and supervisors dealing with performance management will need to have an understanding of this segment of the workforce along with managing regular full-time employees in order to effectively manage their work team.

New Roles in the Team Process

Work Team Process

The workplace is becoming more dynamic and more fluid. Moving away from an outdated vertical organizational structure with its hierarchy of division managers directing work units or departments under the direction of a supervisor, who in turn may delegate certain work responsibilities to group leaders who direct the hourly employees who perform the basic work tasks of the department. New work structures tend to be flatter, with fewer mid-level and low-level managers directing a cadre of supervisors who deal with the employees on the production line or in the warehouse or in the offices. The flatter work structure eliminates many layers of middle managers through which work directions and communications must flow.

More and more, employers are experimenting with the use of workgroups or project teams team made up of employees with various work units in the organization and with a variety of job skills or knowledge needed for the project. The employees are assigned to the project, a project leader is designated, and the individuals interact as needed in a group defining needed work, assigning tasks, interacting throughout the period of the project to achieve the specified results.

These workgroups may be called work teams, employee committees, project teams or other such designations selected by management and/or the work team. Individuals may be assigned full time to the team project or maybe designated to perform a certain proportion of work time to the team and remainder of the time to other teams or to regular work tasks.

Project teams are more than just a staff meeting

Employee committees are an organized process in which a

selected group of employees meet for a specific purpose or to solve a specific problem. The group may be referred to as a committee or a team. Committee members are usually from different jobs, departments, or locations in an organization. Employees from varied work units are selected for committees because they can bring different perspectives and ideas to help solve the problem.

In some organizations, project team participation may be voluntary. In others, management may select or appoint employees to teams. Participation in the committee normally continues until the committee has accomplished its specified purpose

Employee project teams are more than just a staff meeting to discuss workplace issues. Working on a project team requires a high degree of personal organization, communication within the group, sharing of data, information and work output, participating in meetings or communications, and meeting agreed on deadlines for the provision of assigned tasks to the team. For our purpose here, we will use the term project team.

Project teams are successful because they focus on open communication and cooperative relationships between participants. Through open relationships and cooperation, team members may use a variety of communication styles to develop group consensus to solve problems and make decisions.

As a member of a project team, you may become involved in a wide variety of workplace issues. Frequently, employee committees are involved in quality improvement issues. Examples of may include ways to eliminate waste of material or scrap, reduce or prevent errors, eliminate merchandise returns due to poor quality, improve quality measurement, define training needs, reduce complaints or other similar issues.

Productivity and efficiency issues are often a subject of project team discussion. Your committee may be asked to come up with better or faster ways to make your firm's product or provide its services. Project teams may be used to design and launch new products or services into the marketplace or to convert or update software updates that are used in the administration of the business. Other issues frequently addressed by committees include cost control ideas, elimination of waste, reducing accidents, or improving housekeeping.

A self-directed work team is a group of workers who are granted a high degree of autonomy to manage themselves. A self-directed work team works as a group to accomplish assigned tasks in making the firm's products or providing services.

Working as a group, team members set their own production or service schedules, decide work assignments, check work quality or results, and train members. In some organizations, team members also have the authority to select new members, appraise performance, and recommend disciplinary action.

Building team spirit among members is essential

The building of a team spirit among team members is an important element in promoting cooperation and successful results. As team members interact together and develop working relationships to achieve an agreed goal, a team spirit begins to grow. In some organizations, employee committees and teams are given names. The team names help promote interest and loyalty to the team effort.

Employee committees and teams have achieved good results in unionized firms as well as in non-union firms. Unionized firms with successful employee involvement programs have involved union representatives in the planning and development of employee involvement activities. The goal of employee teams and committees is to get employees involved in workplace improvements, not to affect the collective bargaining role of the union.

New Roles

The team process creates new roles in an organization. There are new roles for employees, supervisors, and management. In addition, certain individuals assume new roles as team leaders and team facilitators.

In the team process, team members meet, select their own leader and work cooperatively to solve a specific problem. A Team facilitator coordinates the activities of various teams or committees in the organization. Team or committee members perform their regular job duties in addition to team activities.

In the team process the traditional supervisor-subordinate role changes. The team concept does not require that a supervisor or manager be in charge of the team. Management may designate or select a team leader, or the team may select its own leaders and members are accountable to the team as a whole. A supervisor or manager may participate in a team just like any other employee team member. In some organizations, supervisors are assigned leadership positions in the team process because of their knowledge of technical issues, organizational matters or other problem-solving skills.

A supervisor who assumes a leadership role in a committee may be called upon for his or her expertise to guide fellow team members to identify problems or work towards solutions. In the team process, the supervisor's role changes from "boss" to coach or advisor.

The team leader is an individual selected by team members to serve as a leader and coordinator of team activities. The team leader is responsible to conduct the team meetings, promote participation by all members, coordinate work assignments, train team members, and lead the group to achieve its problem-solving goal. Being selected as a team leader helps an individual to develop skills in leadership, communication, and organization. For many individuals, this represents a new challenge. Rather than just "doing your own job," the team leader is responsible to lead and motivate fellow team members to accomplish committee goals.

A team facilitator is an individual who is responsible for coordinating activities between various committees and management. The team facilitator generally has received formal training in the team process. Often, the team facilitator is responsible to provide training and instruction to individuals who are selected as team leaders.

Team or committee members will be involved in a variety of activities that differ from regular job tasks. As a team member, an employee is actively involved in group discussions to identify specific work problems and suggest ways to solve the problems. Employees also may be involved in developing, maintaining or researching work records related to the problem being studied. In some committees, the employee may be involved in the charting of data, preparing reports of committee recommendations or making presentations to committee members or management.

Designated time periods or limits may be defined for committee activities, such as one hour per week or per month. During the remainder of the workday, the team member is expected to perform regular job duties.

One of the benefits of the team process is the increased problem-solving capability of the group. Because team members come from a variety of backgrounds in the organization, their diversity of ideas helps to achieve solutions to workplace problems.

As a new group is formed, some members may be reluctant to speak out while others may be more forceful or dominate the discussion. Sometimes, an individual may have a hidden agenda - some special issue that he or she wants from the committee process. It may take time for the committee to really begin functioning as a cooperative problem-solving team.

Achieving team unity takes time. In time, group members begin to develop a sense of "us," where "we" are working together to achieve "our" goal.

Work Team Etiquette

All organizations tend to adopt some basic mores of conduct to maintain cooperative working relationships. Likewise, committees and teams function more effectively when members define and agree to abide by some basic operating principles. Some common etiquette guidelines are summarized below.

+ Actively participate to offer ideas.
+ Acknowledge the ideas and suggestions of others.
+ Listen without making judgment or criticism of others.
+ Avoid dominating the discussion; allow others to participate.
+ Build on other's ideas.
+ Ask questions or seek clarification if more information is needed.
+ Carefully consider each proposal.
+ Make a serious effort to resolve problems.
+ Login - attend all committee meetings.

+ Arrive – log in on time and comply with requested deadlines.
+ Complete all work assignments.
+ Cooperate and communicate with fellow team members.
+ Comply with operating rules.
+ Maintain regular job responsibilities.[24]

Virtual Work Teams

A Growing Trend

The team process has evolved in recent years from employee groups meeting in the workplace to address workplace issues like total quality management. Virtual work teams are groups of employees who work interdependently with a shared purpose, functioning across home and work locations using technology to communicate and collaborate. As workplaces became more global, the team process was adapted from location centered meetings to virtual work teams that interacted with other team members through the use of a variety of electronic communication mediums because of their being geographically dispersed.

Another factor that prompts the use of virtual work teams is the fact that many employers have adopted telecommuting procedures to allow employees in certain jobs to work from home on an occasional or part-time or full-time basis. Working as remote employees, these individuals maintain contact with superiors and others in the performance of their duties by logging into the employer computer networks, e-mail and other instant messaging systems as needed. According to the World at Work Total Rewards and Practices survey cited earlier, an overwhelming majority of employers are now offering a variety of workplace flexibility options to employees. World at Work reports that seventy-eight percent (78%) of employers permit ad hoc scheduling of telework or similar home-based work activities. The survey data further details that ongoing part-time telework is permitted by seventy-two percent (72%) of firms and full-time remote work is permitted by fifty-six percent (56%) of firms.[25]

This growing use of remote workers naturally lends itself to the use of virtual work teams as employers implement work improvement or project management tasks from a geographically dispersed workforce. According to Human Resource Management Review, a survey of 1372 business respondents from eighty different countries reported that eighty-five percent (85%) worked on virtual teams and forty-eight percent (48%) reported that work team members were from different cultures.[26]

The growth of virtual work teams has been attributed in part to the events of 9-11.

The use of virtual work teams has taken on a life of its own as a leading management process since the beginning of the new millennium. The growth of virtual work teams has been attributed in part to the events of September 11, 2001, and its effect on the economy and subsequent travel restrictions. Sabre, Inc., the company operating a computerized airline reservation system, began using virtual work teams as early as 1999. As reported in Academy of Management Executive, Sabre switched from functionally based work teams to market-based cross-functional virtual teams creating as many as sixty-five virtual work teams across its home office and field locations in the U.S. and Canada. These team members communicated through e-mail, telephone, video conferencing and web-based conferencing.[27]

Entities setting up virtual work teams design the team process based upon the needs and the structure of the organization. Among factors to consider is the degree of virtuality, reflecting the proportion of time that team members work face to face compared to virtually. In part, this may relate to the number of team members at a given location. Another dimension for virtual work teams is the proportion of time that members are committed to teamwork activities compared to time spent on other non-team work tasks.

Overcoming Concerns

There are some concerns that have been identified relating to the use of virtual work teams. These may include difficulties in maintaining clear and timely communication, inability to promote cooperation and collaboration, greater obstacles in promoting team engagement and trust, and greater challenges in supervising and motivating remote workers.

Authors Jessica Lipnack and Jeffrey Stamps writing in

Strategy & Leadership, assert that the basic principles for promoting success in virtual teams are to address three key facets: purpose, people, and links.

Purpose - The definition of purpose is critical to the success of any organization and particularly so in the formation of virtual work teams. More than a mere mission statement, a virtual team needs a defined purpose and cooperative goals that detail the desired end result(s).

People – The people are the key, the core of the virtual work team. The individual members are selected because of their knowledge or skills and abilities to contribute to achieving the virtual team's goals, balancing their ability to be autonomous and self-reliant while working cooperatively with the team.

Links – The links are communication mediums through which the people interact to achieve the desired purpose. The links significantly rely upon digital technologies, expanding upon the former face to face communications of employees or workplace committees in single site meetings.[28]

Over the years that the team process has been utilized, practitioners have gained experience in what works and identified areas where team leaders need to focus their efforts in order to maintain a high level of productivity and results from virtual team efforts. Some significant points are summarized here.

Leading effective virtual teams requires a skill set that balances people skills with tech skills while possessing an awareness of the subject matter and industry. The traditional supervisor of on-site employees has the opportunity to engage subordinates face to face, individually, in meetings, and even socially outside of the work environment. These visual and verbal interactions, along with observations of the individual's work ethic which include non-verbal communication, form the basis for how the supervisor communicates with and motivates the employee. But these communication elements are absent in the virtual work relationship. The team leader must find other ways to promote team engagement, build trust, and motivate remote workers. Some suggestions are offered here.

Virtual Team Building Tips

There are a number of things individuals and organizations can build effective virtual teams. It begins with defining the goal or purpose of the team. Top management authorizing the use of a virtual team process would normally define the over-riding goal or objective that the team has been formed to address. The definition of this goal will affect the selection of skills needed to input possible solutions and provide a basis to select employees for team participation.

Select the team – Virtual team members may be invited to participate or selected or recruited based upon the defined team goal, knowledge or skills needed, and the culture of the organization. Look for individuals possessing a balance of technical and interpersonal skills.

Clarify systems or communications mediums – Virtual employees may be interacting remotely with the employer's operational software systems on local or wide area networks or cloud technology using appropriate protocols to control access, protect data integrity while facilitating timely communications. Specify required or preferred communication media such as e-mail, video-teleconference software, instant messaging, phone or graphic links. For virtual and remote employees, this may require defining requirements for computer hardware or laptop or tablets possessing data processing capabilities that are compatible with the employer's systems.

Define an expectation of project time and level of involvement – Where employees selected for virtual work team assignments may have other non-team duties, clarify time demands for the team versus non-team activities.

Create an environment of involvement and inclusiveness - Invite team member participation in clarifying goals, processes. Getting team members to further define the team's goals or operating processes or measures of results creates a greater sense of participation and ownership of the efforts and results of the team.

Elicit input for defining team performance measures – Building from the defined team goal or objective(s), seek input from team members to clarify and define benchmarks which can serve as measures of results achieved. Consider measures for team performance as well as individual contributions and performance.

Seek to identify or create performance measurement data sources - Establish measures for tracking qualitative and quantitative aspects of individual and team performance outcomes. In some cases, existing financial or operational data sources may be tracked to measure the effectiveness of project results. In cases where new systems or procedures are created, new tracking measures will need to be defined and implemented.

Actively seek to build consensus-based decisions – A virtual team consists of members with expertise in various subject matters related to the project goal or mission. The team's decision-making process should actively elicit input from all members, evaluate the pros and cons, weigh issues and priorities, and seek to achieve a consensus to resolve issues. The team can then make its recommendations to management or implement new processes in line with its specified mission.

Seek to build trust within the team – Absent the interpersonal relationship for building trust or building opportunities for face to face interactions, team leaders can encourage trust among members by promoting timely communication patterns and consistency in interactions. Trust will grow with timely communications and accomplishments.

Provide feedback to team members – Follow-up and feedback communication by the team leader to team members is an essential ingredient in promoting inclusion in a virtual working environment. The feedback that acknowledges team member inputs or contributions provides recognition for the effort. Feedback seeking clarification regarding a team member's input helps to ensure understanding without drawing conclusions or making judgments.

Consider opportunities for face to face meeting(s) – Face to face interaction between team leaders and team members can be particularly valuable in the team selection phase, initial training and project startup -launch phases. Such meetings provide an opportunity for social interaction and putting a face to the voice. The use of audio-visual teleconference mediums likewise offers a similar opportunity.

Maintain Connections in Age of Isolation

Addressing the issue of the growing number of employees who work virtually outside of a central office, Reuters reporter Lauren

Young recently interviewed Dan Schwabel, author of "Back to Human: How Great Leaders Create Connection in the Age of Isolation." Author Schawbel reports that one-third of workers in the U.S. often work remotely. These employees often rely on e-mail communication to keep in touch with co-workers and superiors in the central office, but many often feel lonely, missing the social connection of work and lack a feeling of engagement. There is a trade-off for the flexibility of working from home and one effect is the feeling of isolation. Such isolation can be a significant cause of employee job separations because of loneliness and low engagement.[29]

One-third of workers in the U.S often work remotely.

One challenge for project team leaders then is to keep remote team members engaged. Schawbel suggests that remote employees will work harder if they have a sense of connection. For example, a project team leader may let a remote worker lead a virtual team meeting. Another suggestion is to maximize the use of video conferencing systems which provide an opportunity for participants to see and hear fellow team members. When employees participate in a video teleconference, there is a greater likelihood of dressing appropriately for a workplace meeting.

Another element that makes for a positive employment

experience is the ability to cultivate friendships at work. In the absence of building face to face friendships, the virtual worker can build relationships with team members through regular team communications. While video communication cannot fully equate to face to face interactions at work, it is important for video conference participants to put down the cell phone with its distracting outside messages in order to fully participate in the meeting at hand.

Summary

Virtual work teams have grown to play an integral role in a more participatory management style of many progressive employers in recent years. The growing use of electronic communications mediums coupled with greater numbers of telecommuting employees has contributed to the rise of this management practice. But, managing virtual workers is substantially different from managing employees in a central office work site. Creative new leadership practices are needed to select, train, direct and motivate a diverse group of employees from a wide variety of job specialties, locations, and differing perspectives.

Managing Employee Performance

Managing Performance Promotes Productivity

Entities that hire employees have a concern that those employees are performing adequately. Traditionally, employers have used some sort of performance appraisal process, and survey data cited earlier reveals that an overwhelming percentage of entities use a formal process to manage employee performance. But, recently, the traditional formal performance appraisal has come under fire according to journal articles and news reports. Yet, even where such reports cite stories of leading employers dropping the old fashioned annual formal performance appraisal, it has been replaced by some alternate process for communicating performance expectations and managing results. Clearly, the bottom line remains; that managers want the employee hired to do a job to perform that job well, and there is a need for some sort of tool or process to communicate expectations and provide feedback on results.

In researching data related to Achieving Performance Results, we sought to examine a variety of performance management resources that enhance the reader's ability to convey performance expectations, seek to motivate employees, and where necessary deal with performance problems. The concepts and ideas outlined here will be useful regardless of whether your firm uses annual performance appraisal or another process for providing performance feedback to employees.

Team Leader's Responsibilities

One of the primary responsibilities of a team leader or supervisor is to direct the activities of subordinate employees to accomplish specified tasks. Among those responsibilities are activities related to communicating, motivating, and directing subordinates. These are skills that often are the most difficult for newly appointed team leaders or supervisors. Many supervisors are promoted to their jobs because of their superior technical skills. However, without additional training on dealing with "people" issues, some newly appointed supervisors experience considerable difficulty in adjusting to their new role.

The team leader or supervisor is the main link between Company management and the employee workgroup. Communicating work requirements and providing feedback or evaluating results is an important leadership activity. This activity forms the basis for the performance management process. Because of the close daily working relationship with operating employees, some supervisors tend to feel more loyalty toward the workgroup rather than upper management. As a result, critical evaluation of team members or subordinates may be seen as an unpleasant task.

Purpose of Performance Management

Performance management is a process of creating a workplace where employees are enabled to perform to the best of their abilities. It is not a once a year discussion. Rather, it is continuous communication conveying expectations, providing guidance to maximize performance and feedback on results. Performance management includes many or all of the following elements:

Define Performance Expectations – An important first step in performance management is to define performance expectations, clarifying what tasks or accomplishments are expected. Performance expectations are normally defined in terms of tasks accomplished including considerations relating to timelines, deadlines, outcomes, quality or quantity of work accomplishment.

Performance Feedback - Performance feedback provides an opportunity for the team leader or supervisor to assess the employee's job performance during a specified period and provide feedback to the employee. The result of the discussion on job performance should improve understanding between employee and team leader or supervisor regarding job responsibilities and performance expectations.

Whether this is done through one or more informal

feedback discussions or a periodic performance evaluation, it gets the employee and supervisor together and talking. It is a way to provide performance feedback. In the absence of a scheduled discussion, there is often very little performance feedback to the employee. If the supervisor is too busy to talk, the employee, typically assumes that performance is okay. The other common occurrence is that the employee only hears complaints when something goes wrong. Neither alternative promotes a good understanding of job expectations.

Correct Poor Performance - Another important purpose of performance management is to correct poor performance. Corrective performance discussions can be scheduled at any time when it becomes necessary to advise the employee of performance problems and to specify corrective action. Every Human Resource specialist can relate a story about a supervisor who fired an employee for poor performance with no record on file of any performance problems or disciplinary warnings.

Coach for Improved Performance - An important challenge for supervisors is to motivate employees to further improve job performance. Through coaching and advice, the supervisor can offer suggestions to the employee on better or more efficient ways of performing job duties. Through a systematic assessment of the employee's skills and abilities, the team leader or supervisor can identify job assignments to provide broader experiences or new challenges for the employee.

Training needs assessment – The measurement of an employee's current performance and identification of performance improvement needs serves to target training needs for the individual. Poor or marginal performance may be corrected by training to enhance or upgrade the employee's job knowledge or skills.

Justify Pay Adjustments - Employee performance ratings can be used as a basis for making salary adjustments. The correlation of pay adjustments to performance ratings puts a pay for performance philosophy into practice. Performance management can also serve as an objective basis to determine bonus or incentive payouts for eligible employees.

Succession Planning – Performance management provides an opportunity to evaluate current workforce abilities and interests to identify candidates for future leadership roles in the organization. The performance evaluation process can not only assess results in the employee's current role but can also elicit career interests and identify the employee's suitability for other roles in the organization.

Evaluate Candidates for Promotion - The performance discussion serves as an excellent process to identify employee career interests and evaluate candidates for promotion. The employee's record of achievements, performance strengths and weaknesses provide added insights for a supervisor considering candidates for promotion.

Document Personnel Actions – A record of performance management discussions helps to document personnel decisions such as promotions, pay increases, transfers, demotions, or discharges. In the event of subsequent legal proceedings, such as a discrimination claim or wrongful discharge lawsuit, documented personnel actions help to justify management decisions in defense of the claim.

Benefits of Performance Management

The major benefit of a performance management process is the employee's improved understanding of job requirements, which helps promote better job performance. When a team leader or supervisor provides feedback on employee performance, it contributes to helping the organization to be more productive, reducing errors, improving quality, and promoting better efficiency.

Entities that define a pay-performance correlation have a more objective basis to administer employee pay. Without a performance management process in place, there is a greater possibility of failing to achieve fair and equitable pay adjustments for all employees. Further, there is an objective basis for avoiding bias in pay adjustments.

Illustrative Case Example
"A Sobering Situation"

The owner of an industrial product distributing firm took pride in providing a work environment in which management cared for employees and their families. This paternalistic management style was ineffective, however, when it was necessary to correct an employee's drinking problem. The employee refused to acknowledge that drinking was a problem. The owner was reluctant to take corrective action against the employee who was also a personal friend for 15 years. If the problem were not addressed, customer or public safety could be jeopardized creating serious liability for the firm.

Management examined the alternatives for dealing with this matter and evidence of other performance problems was also found. The firm's executives elected to implement a performance feedback process for all employees. Key performance guidelines were developed to deal objectively with performance issues including those of the problem employee. The performance feedback discussion showing the seriousness of the problem prompted the employee to seek treatment for alcoholism.

The performance feedback process helped to identify and correct other problem issues in the workgroup, resulting in the retention of valued employees whose knowledge and experience were assets in the customer-focused business.

***

Importance of Management Commitment

One essential ingredient in a successful performance management process is executive management commitment. If top managers in the organization are too busy to actively participate in planning, implementation, and administration of performance management efforts, then the process will be only marginally effective at best. On the other hand, when team leaders or supervisors see top managers actively involved in an implementation training session and then providing performance feedback on a timely basis, the team leaders and supervisors will follow the example set by management.

Defining Your Policy

It is recommended that the organization's performance management process be defined in a written policy and procedure guideline for supervisors and managers. If the organization has an employee handbook, then certain aspects of the policy may be included in the handbook to communicate information to employees. A sample policy appears in the Appendix.

Interpreting Your Policy

Written policy guidelines facilitate a more consistent interpretation of policy information by team leaders and supervisors. In the absence of any written guidelines, then verbal instructions and training of supervisors are essential to promote an understanding of the performance management process.

Whether an organization's policies are written or verbal, a major goal should be consistent policy administration. Performance and pay administration issues are a key area where employees are quick to note favoritism, inconsistent ratings, or other unfair actions. The timely scheduling of performance or feedback discussions to coincide with your organization's policy is important to maintain good employee relations. If your policy states that feedback occurs quarterly or another specified interval, the team leader or supervisor should make a concerted effort to arrange a performance discussion with the employee on time. Whether a performance review schedule is published in an employee handbook or based upon past practice, it creates an expectation by employees. Failure to meet the schedule causes employee concerns.

Explain Performance Management to New Employees

An effective process to orientate new employees to the workplace substantially aids in their effectiveness on the job. In addition to usual employee orientation issues, this is a good time to acquaint the employee with the organization's performance management process. In entities that correlate pay and performance, a discussion of performance management issues helps to emphasize the importance of the pay for performance objective. An employee who understands the firm's performance evaluation and pay process is more likely to perform better.

Summary

Managing employee performance is an essential responsibility of a team leader, supervisor or manager. The real challenge to the supervisor is to find ways to motivate workers and then to evaluate their work on the job.

Team leaders, supervisors, and managers face new challenges as the workforce evolves and becomes more diverse. Greater workforce participation by minorities, women, single parents, and older workers will result in differing needs and interests by employees. Further, as a wider variety of contingent and alternative workforce arrangements have become commonplace, there may be different practices or procedures to be observed because of the different work relationships.

Performance management has long been recognized by human resource professionals to be an essential management tool. Even though most managers advocate for a pay for performance work philosophy, the actual usage of objective performance measures sometimes falls short.

The performance management process is designed to promote better understanding between team leader, supervisor, and employee, in relation to job responsibilities and performance expectations. Active support of top management is an essential element in a successful performance management program.

Defining Employee Responsibilities

To effectively manage performance, there must first be an understanding between employee and the team leader or supervisor about job responsibilities. Without clear direction from the team leader or supervisor, the employee will learn job duties from fellow workers or struggle along on a trial and error basis.

Onboarding of new employees is an important starting point for clarifying job responsibilities. The new employee's orientation should be more than a quick introduction to coworkers or assignment of a desk or workstation. To be effective, the orientation should include a detailed discussion of job duties as well as an explanation of the organization's policies and benefits. One tool that is useful in this process is the job description.

The Job Description

The job description is a brief written summary of the duties and responsibilities of a job or team member assignment. The job description helps to organize work functions, define relationships between jobs, list job tasks and duties, and clarify the level of responsibility or authority.

Job descriptions are typically one, two, or three pages in length, depending on the scope of job responsibilities and the degree of detail desired by management. Job descriptions can be prepared in a variety of formats. However, job descriptions typically include the following elements:

Job Title - The name of the job.

Job Summary - A one or two-sentence summary that defines the job's overall function.

Job qualification - A brief listing of educational & experience qualifications needed to perform the job.

Duties and Responsibilities - A listing of essential job functions and tasks.

Working environment/physical demands – A listing of the physical and/or mental demands of the job together with a description of working conditions and environment.

Using Job Descriptions

The job description need not be feared as a bureaucratic demon created by the Human Resource Department to limit management discretion or to provide the employee with a ready-made excuse to say, "That's not my job." Rather, the job description is a useful management tool that can help promote good employee relations and make the team leader or supervisor's job much easier.

When job descriptions are defined, the team leader or supervisor has a handy reference for dealing with many personnel management issues which arise, such as the following:

Define Job Duties: Job descriptions help to organize work functions and assign tasks to various jobs. Defining job duties is particularly useful when an organization is changing due to growth, reduction in size, reorganization, or the introduction of new procedures or technology. Listing the duties serves to clarify the essential functions of the job. A concise listing of duties helps management to reorganize or reassign tasks and to make sure that responsibility is assigned for all job functions.

Define Job Relationships: Job descriptions help to clarify how each job interacts with other jobs, by defining the nature of contacts, authority, and supervision given or received.

A job description can be an important document in defending an employment decision in an employment discrimination claim.

Training and Orientation of new workers: The job description provides a ready-made outline to orient the new employee to job responsibilities. Training for employees on work procedures or job skills can also be developed based upon the job description.

Communication of Job Responsibilities: Throughout the employment relationship, a job description serves as the standard of reference for defining the employee's job responsibilities. A properly prepared job description is the supervisor's best defense against the employee who tries to shirk a job assignment by saying, "That's not my job."

Recruiting and Selecting: The job description can be an invaluable aid in recruiting and selecting new employees. Job description details are useful in specifying work qualifications, in evaluating resumes or applications, and in determining interview questions. According to the Americans with Disabilities Act of 1990, an employee's written job description, prepared before advertising or interviewing for the job is considered to be evidence of the essential functions of the job.

Evaluating Performance: The job description provides a

ready list of what tasks the employee should be performing. Referring to the job description, the team leader or supervisor can then rate how well the employee performs assigned tasks.

Wage-Hour Law Compliance: the job description is an important basis for documenting job responsibilities to classify jobs as exempt from federal and state wage-hour laws. The Fair Labor Standards Act, for example, exempts executive, professional, administrative, outside sales and certain computer positions from overtime pay, and timekeeping requirements.

Pay Determination: Human resources and compensation specialists use job descriptions to determine pay structures and pay ranges for jobs. Job descriptions are an important basis for comparing company pay rates to area salary surveys to assure that pay levels are competitive.

Preparing Job Descriptions

The team leader or supervisor who directs the job activities of a position is normally best suited for preparing job descriptions for those jobs under his or her direction. This task may be assigned to the team leader. Some organizations have found that employee involvement in the preparation of job descriptions helps promote employee interest and understanding of job responsibilities. In either case, it is recommended that job descriptions be edited by a human resource specialist to avoid any discriminatory statements and to assure consistency in format, content, and style.

Here are some suggestions to aid the team leader or supervisor in preparing effective job descriptions:

+ List major tasks and duties performed in the job.
+ Avoid detailed lists of specific job procedures. Rather, describe the functions, responsibilities, and activities performed.
+ Take care to define the responsibilities of the job, not the characteristics of the individual in the job.
+ Identify the nature or form of instructions received and the scope of decisions made on the job.
+ Identify computer hardware devices, software applications and communications media used in performing job duties.
+ Identify any equipment, systems, or tools operated and typical tasks performed using the equipment.

+ Identify whether the job tasks must be performed at a central job site location or whether tasks may be performed remotely.

+ Describe the nature of communications and contacts with others. Indicate whether contacts are with the workgroup, to other departments, outside the organization, with customers or vendors, etc.

+ Describe whether the position requires the incumbent to function independently, exercise initiative, comply with guidelines or policies, or perform limited tasks that are closely monitored by others.

+ Use action verbs to describe functions and activities. Examples include: plans, develops, supervises, directs, recommends, operates, sets up, tends, etc.

+ Avoid titles or terms that are gender-specific.

+ Identify the working environment for the job and physical or mental demands placed on an employee performing job tasks.

+ Follow your organization's established format for style, organization, and length of job descriptions.

Sample Job Description

A sample job description is reproduced below:

JOB DESCRIPTION
Customer Service Associate

SUMMARY: Under general supervision, the Customer Service Associate is responsible for maintaining a positive customer experience by telephone and electronic communication accessing a proprietary inventory management system to identify customer needs, providing pricing and quotes, entering and processing orders for established accounts, setting up new accounts, monitoring inventory levels, resolving customer problems and performing related tasks.

REPORTS TO: Customer Service Manager

QUALIFICATIONS:

* High school education, preferably supplemented by advanced training in call-center and/or office operations procedures and business skills comparable to an associate's degree.

* 2-4 years' experience in customer service or call center operations.

49

* Possess an understanding of inventory management or ERP or SAP systems and MS Office software.

* Demonstrate abilities to deal professionally with internal and external customers, handling customer service and order entry procedures, excellent telephone skills, ability to handle work activity in a fast-paced environment.

* Any other equivalent combination of training and experience.

ESSENTIAL DUTIES AND RESPONSIBILITIES:

1. Receives customer inquiries by e-mail, telephone, postal mail, or other mediums. Exercises tact and professional demeanor to maintain a positive customer experience to identify customer needs and efficiently service the needs. May handle status queries, sales quotes, orders, sample requests, returns, credits or other order adjustments. Evaluates order requirements, verifies accuracy of data and contacts customer or superior in the event of a discrepancy. Operates a computer terminal to enter order data to a proprietary inventory management system. Enters data to change orders when necessary. Records notes or special instructions on order as necessary to assure proper handling of the order by others. Performs tasks according to company operating policies, procedures, and defined performance standards.

2. Sets up and creates new customer files in the system, coordinating with credit, finance, or sales department personnel as needed. Confers with superior to identify the need for special procedures or inventory control processes. Creates files, procedures, and reports as needed to properly administer orders.

3. Receives customer telephone or e-mail inquiries regarding the status of orders or deliveries. Checks order status and provides timely reports of information to the customer. Communicates order information or changes between departments. May research system information to solve routine problems related to order information, changes, status, or delivery, and provides timely communication to the customer. May provide information about product availability or established prices.

4. May compose and send e-mail or text or letter correspondence using proper grammar, sentence structure, and punctuation.

5. May operate other office equipment as needed to supply information to internal or external customers, including the use of computer printers, copiers, facsimile, telephone or other devices as needed.

6. Operates desktop computer terminal, tablet or other input devices to access data, enter data, and change or delete data as necessary according to prescribed procedures for inventory management and order processing. Selects prescribed screen format, follows menu cues and reads or enters data as necessary. May refer to computer reference manual or superior in the event of computer entry difficulty. May operate computer system to upload data to the cloud or other back-up media.

7. May perform tasks from remote or home-based worksite subject to management approval and confirmation of suitable secure telecommunications are established. May provide reports as specified related to remote work assignments.

8. May perform related duties or fill in for others in the department or other departments when requested. May train or instruct fellow workers regarding own duties. Fills in at switchboard in the absence of Receptionist/Switchboard Attendant.

9. Performs special projects or tasks when requested by superior. May participate in project or work teams performing tasks relating to work team activity or the mission.

10. Periodically checks work area and maintains a neat and orderly work area. Observes company policies related to dress, appearance, attendance, employment, etc.

11. Performs tasks in an office or remote environment as authorized. Tasks require light to moderate exertion and dexterity to operate office equipment, maintain records and communicate with others.

12. Performs other duties as assigned. Job duties are subject to change as directed by management.

Illustrative Case Example
"... Who's on First?"

A successful high-tech equipment manufacturer was experiencing rapid growth. To respond to increasing customer demands, there were frequent staff additions and the reassignment of job responsibilities. Some changes, however, were made too quickly causing employee confusion and affecting customer response capabilities.

A newly hired product designer quit in frustration exclaiming, "There's no organization here! Nobody knows what they're doing!" Then, two customer service clerks argued over responsibility for a major account allowing several other orders to go unfilled.

Customer complaints to top management prompted action. The firm brought in an outside consultant to remedy the situation. To clarify job responsibilities, the consultant developed job descriptions for each job. The systematic listing of job duties eliminated confusion, improved employee understanding of responsibilities, and aided management to effectively plan controlled growth in this expanding industry.

***

Keep Job Descriptions Current

The job description is a management tool with many uses. As with other equipment or machine, the job description also requires periodic maintenance as new systems or processes are introduced. A team leader or supervisor should keep a current job description for each job supervised. As job duties or work activities change, the job description should be reviewed and revised to reflect these changes. Also, check the job description whenever hiring a new employee. Make sure that job duties are current and that job qualifications are reasonable and job-related.

Job descriptions can become evidence at a hearing or a trial. For this reason, accurate job descriptions are an important part of a company's defense in cases of discrimination allegations or wrongful discharge claims.

Job Crafting

Job crafting is the term that describes the practice of tailoring a job's duties around the unique skills and abilities of a particular

52

employee or new hire. Often, experienced workers possess very unique job knowledge or skills and a hiring manager wants to maximize the mutual benefit of designing a job that will best fit the individual as well as meet the needs of the organization. Significant changes to a job description may justify changes to the job's pay rate or range. Such factors can be a significant factor in retaining an experienced employee or in recruiting an individual whose background brings important experience to the job.

Summary

The job description is a brief written summary of the duties and responsibilities of the job. The job description is a useful management tool that can aid the supervisor in defining job duties and relationships, recruiting and selecting workers, orientating new workers, appraising performance, and more.

When preparing job descriptions, describe the duties of the job and not the abilities or activities of an incumbent. Use action verbs to describe work functions, machines operated, authority for decisions, or types of contacts with others. Be sure to update job descriptions as job responsibilities change.

Setting Performance Objectives

Importance of Objective Measurement

Once the job description has been prepared to define what tasks are performed, the next step in a performance management process is to identify how well the tasks should be performed.

To have a fair measure of the employee's performance, there must be a standard or basis for comparison. When the team leader or supervisor has defined performance objectives for each job, the employee's performance can be evaluated against a standard. Performance objectives can be defined on any significant activity related to the individual job, project, and correlated to the goals or mission of the entity.

Clearly defined performance objectives help the employee to better understand job duties and priorities. A performance objective or standard specifies for the employee what is a desired level of performance. In the absence of defined performance objectives, the employee most likely will work at his or her own pace or conform to the norms of the workgroup.

Why Define Objectives?

Unfortunately, too many team leaders or supervisors attempt to evaluate their employee's job performance without defining clear performance standards. Their reasoning may go like this: "I rate my people on a gut feeling," or "Knowledge jobs are hard to quantify "or "There are too many variables on this job. Standards work better for factory positions where the work is repetitive." The unfortunate result of this attitude is that the team leader or supervisor most likely will fail to have a clear picture of the employee's performance.

The foundation of performance management is to use accomplishment-based performance measures. Without performance measures, performance management is a purely subjective opinion. There is a greater likelihood of rater bias.

Benefits of Performance Objectives

The performance management process, because it is administered by humans, is subject to a degree of subjectivity. The use of job-related work performance objectives or standards helps to assure the following benefits:

+ Improved objectivity in performance measures.
+ Greater consistency in performance measures.
+ Detailing of job priorities.
+ Clearly defined basis for comparing an employee's job performance to specified standards.
+ Clearer understanding by an employee of important job responsibilities and priorities.
+ Defined performance "targets" which will promote greater productivity, quality, attendance, etc.
+ Accurate documentation of poor performance to justify corrective action or dismissal to reduce the potential liability of legal claims by current or former employees.

Defining Performance Objectives

Several years ago, management by objectives, or MBO, emerged as a popular management theory. Under formal MBO plans, organization objectives were developed and sub-objectives were defined for each level of the organization down to the individual. Whether your organization undertakes a formal MBO program or adopts a less formal approach, performance objectives are an important element in the performance management process.

The team leader or supervisor may elect to define objectives for a variety of performance factors such as: meeting work task deadlines, timely response to communications, project completion, quantity of work performed, quality or accuracy of work, control of costs, completing tasks within specified deadlines, accomplishment of specified projects or tasks, or other similar performance objectives.

The performance objective should be attainable but should require some extra effort on the part of the employee. The performance objective should be measurable. To measure performance, the supervisor and/or employee must maintain some basic records of work output to measure results and provide a basis to determine the attainment of objectives.

SMART Objective Setting

The term SMART serves as an acronym for defining performance goals, as noted below:

Specific – clear and understandable

Measurable – verifiable and results-oriented

Attainable – yet sufficiently challenging

Relevant – to the mission of the department or organization,

Time-Bound – with a schedule and specific milestones.

Measurement Period

The period for measuring performance objectives will depend upon two factors -- the work activity being measured and the organization's defined performance measures. For work activities that can be measured in hourly or daily or weekly periods, a monthly or quarterly summary of performance compared objective may be suitable. For projects or deadline activities, the project completion may be the appropriate measurement period. For long term performance goals, interim goals or performance checkpoints are recommended.

Performance Standards

Engineered standards are used by some manufacturing entities to define performance requirements for incentive or piece-rate compensation plans. These plans are developed by industrial engineers. The industrial engineer performs time and motion study to determine performance standards that are used to compute incentive or piece-rate pay procedures. While engineered performance standards are typically used in repetitive or mass production environments, these concepts may be applied to other environments as well.

Employee Participation

Involve employees and team members in the process of goal setting. Elicit employee thoughts on ways to measure job results and success, as well as factors that may hinder goal achievement. Recognize employee input and use it as a basis that promotes two-way communication and offers solutions to overcome perceived barriers to goal attainment.

Getting Employee Commitment

Getting your employees to agree to a performance goal promotes their commitment to attaining the goal. When defining performance goals, solicit employee input on what job activities may be indicators of performance and what constitutes a good performance. A one on one discussion is recommended when defining individual performance objectives. Individual or small group discussions are recommended when eliciting departmental or workgroup goals.

Sample Performance Objectives

To assist the team leader and supervisor in defining objectives, some sample performance objectives appear below:

Sample Performance Objective (Performance Factor Measured)

+ Respond to E-mails or Messaging within one day. (Meeting deadline)

+ Enter time reporting entries by the end of each workday. (Timeliness or reporting)

+ Complete sales analysis within two days of the month-end. (Meeting deadline)

+ Process 100 claims weekly (Quantity of work)

+ Compute pricing and enter 75 orders daily. (Quantity of work)

+ Perform all service calls within 105% of the estimate for time and material. (Cost control and efficiency)

+ Complete the XYZ job by October 31. (Meeting deadline)

+ Maintain on-time attendance for 98% of scheduled work hours. (Attendance control)

+ Answer all telephone calls by the third ring. (Customer service)

+ Reduce overtime hours by 50%. (Cost control)

+ Increase market share to 20%. (Sales productivity)

+ Reduce accounts receivable aging average from 60 to 45 days. (Cost control)

+ Maintain daily sales average of $450.00. (Sales productivity)

+ Clean work area at end of shift. (Safety)

+ Obtain a 2% reduction in material cost without compromising quality. (Cost control)

+ Produce 800 parts per day with not more than a 2% reject rate. (Quantity and Quality)

+ Zero defects - prevent or catch and correct all errors before the product is shipped to the customer. (Quality of work)

+ Ship all standard orders within 24 hours (or 1 business day) of receipt. (Meeting deadline)

Performance Records

The definition of performance goals starts the performance measurement process. To monitor performance results, some basic work records are needed. Often, performance information is obtainable from existing business or accounting records or system data. Be sure to evaluate the availability of relevant records or data when defining performance goals.

In the absence of suitable performance measurement data, examine existing database elements to consider the feasibility of developing or modifying data elements that provide a suitable record to track the employee's achievements against the goal. The record-keeping process should be simple and easy to maintain. Remember to focus on true performance measures. Avoid creating excessive or unnecessary record keeping requirements that may merely track activities.

Record keeping is essential in defining performance goals and tracking results.

Changing Conditions

Sometimes, changing business conditions, staff levels, organizational priorities, or other factors can prevent an employee from meeting performance goals. In such cases, significant factors beyond an employee's control may be viewed as mitigating circumstances. When business conditions or changing priorities adversely affect the work activity, the changing of performance objectives midway during an evaluation may be appropriate. This decision becomes a judgment call by the manager or supervisor. Frequent changing of goals is an indicator of poor planning and inadequate goal setting. Therefore, changing of performance goals "midstream" is discouraged.

Illustrative Case Example
"Movin' On Up"

Upon graduation from school two women, Susan and Carol joined a large company in the area. Both had similar skills and were assigned to comparable administrative jobs. Within two years, each had been promoted to supervisory responsibilities in different areas of the company.

The company introduced a performance management system keyed to its strategic planning and goal-setting process. As a supervisor, Carol grudgingly worked through the goal-setting process and dreaded the performance discussions with employees in her department. Susan, however, had a different perspective. An avid list maker with a drive to work until the job is finished, Susan relished the challenge of setting goals, striving for results, and challenging her subordinates through performance management discussions.

Several years later at a service awards dinner, Carol received her five-year pin. Susan, now a regional manager, was presented with a meritorious performance award for superior achievements. In accepting her award, Susan credited the goal setting and feedback from the firm's performance management plan as an aid in her many achievements.

***

Summary

When a supervisor defines performance goals there is an objective basis for evaluating the employee's performance against a measurable standard. Performance targets aid the employee in focusing efforts to accomplish desired results. Employee commitment is an important element in the goal-setting process. Certain performance records are needed as a basis to measure and evaluate performance.

Getting Ready

Onboarding

The performance management process really begins at the time of hire. The orientation of new employees is an important factor in helping the new worker to be productive. Orientation can be handled personally by the supervisor, or in many cases, portions of the orientation may be delegated to the team leader. The team leader or supervisor should check the employee's progress in learning job tasks and organization procedures. Inadequate orientation and training can be a significant cause of poor performance.

The onboarding process should be a key element in the formation of a new work team. Work team mission and goals, communications protocols, and task-oriented processes are examples of things to cover when onboarding members to a new project team. As time passes and new team members are added to the team, the new members should receive a similar onboarding orientation.

Some firms consider the initial period of employment to be a probationary period. Often, they conduct a performance review at the end of the employee's orientation or probation. In the event of performance problems, the supervisor should deal with these issues promptly by providing further instruction or disciplinary warnings as deemed appropriate. In cases of serious misconduct or grossly poor performance, it is advisable to take immediate corrective action rather than to wait until the end of the orientation or probation period.

Creating a Culture of Feedback

One of the criticisms of a practice of conducting an annual performance appraisal is that the supervisor may at year-end surprise the employee with a bad performance review filled with criticism and resulting in denial or reduction of a pay adjustment or worse yet, the threat of discharge. Team leaders or supervisors fear performance discussions and employees fear feedback and worry about the worst-case scenario denied pay increase or even job loss. Executive Bas Kohnke, writing an article for HRZone.com proposes that fear of feedback can be overcome by creating a culture built on self-compassion. Kohnke says that individuals with greater self-compassion are less likely to be judgmental about their own failures and are therefore better able to accept feedback.

According to Kohnke, a performance management practice with regular feedback creates opportunities to learn. He suggests that regularly providing feedback, presented with compassion, helps the presenter and the employee through difficult conversations that can occur in the performance management process. The key is to present information in a way that shows understanding and helps to find a constructive takeaway.[30]

Daily Performance Feedback

Daily performance feedback is essential to let your employees know where they stand. When a supervisor responds to performance issues as they occur, there is an opportunity to recognize employees for achievements or to provide instructions in the event of errors. Immediate feedback can encourage desired behavior results and reduce the likelihood of repeated performance problems.

Daily performance feedback only needs to be a brief comment, perhaps a minute or two in length. It can be recognition for a job well done, such as: "You did a good job on the Anderson Report," or "I appreciate your efforts in staying late to complete the inventory."

Likewise, a minute or two of advice or instruction will help prevent the recurrence of many performance problems. For example: "I've noticed that the order entry error report has grown recently. Most of the errors appear to be incorrect product codes. Perhaps you can reduce these errors by working from the catalog as you enter orders."

Daily performance feedback by the supervisor will help improve performance because employees will have a better understanding of performance requirements. Do not avoid performance discussions during the year only to "dump" on the employee at performance review time. This practice is unfair to the employee, contributes to ill will, and fails to prevent recurrence of errors.

Addressing Misconduct

Misconduct can be distinguished from job performance problems. Misconduct is typically inappropriate employee behavior which may not be directly related to the actual performance of job duties. Common examples of misconduct are lateness, absenteeism, inappropriate dress or appearance, or poor attitude. Examples of serious misconduct can include theft, falsification of records, or refusal to perform assigned tasks. Suggestions for dealing with misconduct appear at a later section of this book.

Timely Performance Feedback

Conducting timely performance feedback is one simple and important task which the team leader or supervisor can do to maintain the credibility of the performance management process. When you are late in providing performance feedback, the employee assumes everything is OK. This practice can cause poor performance to continue unabated and likely create greater problems for the entity.

If your organization's policy is to conduct a performance discussion on a designated date, be sure to conduct feedback discussions on time. An easy way to keep track of performance discussion due dates is to set up a tickler file. All computer software comes with a calendar feature and schedule reminders. It is a simple task to mark due dates for yourself and the employee who will receive the performance feedback.

Preparing for the Performance Discussion

When preparing the feedback or scheduled performance discussion, take a few minutes to check Company records which may indicate how well or how poorly the employee has performed. You may find useful information from the following:

Operations Records - Every organization has some kinds of records on sales, orders, services rendered, parts produced, costs, or other similar business activities. This data can be a good source of objective information to aid in evaluating employee performance.

Project reports – When a work team is working on a project or evaluating a work practice or analyzing data, such activity likely will be documented in some form of data or narrative report or drafts of reports. Such report documents may provide data or information reflecting contributions by team members thereby providing a record of the employee's contribution to the project or team effort.

Project or work team communications – internal and external communications by e-mail or messaging systems will provide a record of frequency, timeliness, and nature of communications which can be a measure of an employee's contribution to the project or team effort.

Performance Feedback notes – refer to any recent performance feedback discussion notes to see if issues discussed during a prior feedback have continued or if prior identified problems have been corrected.

Quality Records - Records, tests, or inspection reports by your quality assurance personnel are an important performance indicator. Similarly, records on customer returns should be evaluated.

Attendance Records - Company attendance or time records will show how may absences or tardies the employee has had during the past 6 months or year.

Accident Reports - Company records regarding accidents can be an indicator of how well the employee is following safety practices.

Customer Correspondence - When the Company receives correspondence or electronic communication from customers, whether it is compliments or complaints, this information should be relayed back to the employee(s) who worked on the job. Such information may be used to support or document employee performance or performance problems.

Disciplinary Warning Notices - Any disciplinary warning notices issued during the reporting period can be noted as part of the performance management process.

Job Description - The employee's job description outlines what tasks are to be performed. Using the job description as a guide, the supervisor can provide a thorough rating of how well or how poorly each job task listed on the description is being performed.

Performance Goals - As described in an earlier section of this book, a listing of performance goals provides a clear basis to compare performance results to goals.

Performance Rating Guidelines - Always refer to any policies, procedures, or performance rating definitions if provided by your employer.

In summary, try to use these objective facts along with your personal observations and opinions formed during day-to-day communications with the employee.

Examples of Work Records Useful in Preparing for Performance Discussions

+ Project reports or drafts
+ Data analysis relating to job tasks or work team projects
+ Quality records, parts rejected or reworked
+ Response time to communications
+ Timeliness of completing tasks or projects
+ Frequency of meeting deadlines or promise dates
+ Absences, tardies on-time records or attendance records
+ Control or reduction of costs
+ Control or reduction of supplies
+ Ratios comparing quality and quantity
+ Number of errors, computer-generated error or audit reports
+ Costs compared to budgets
+ Costs compared to quotes
+ Ratio comparing work activity to the expected norm
+ Customer correspondence
+ Product returns
+ Order processing time
+ Inventory level
+ Value of inventory
+ Inventory turns
+ Accident reports
+ Inspection or testing reports
+ Scrap or waste reports
+ Orders or claims received or processed
+ Productivity records
+ Number of parts produced per hour or day
+ Number of service calls
+ Material used or consumed

Understand Your Firm's Policy

It is important that the supervisor or manager administer performance discussions in a manner that is consistent with the firm's practice or formal policy. If your firm has a written policy or procedure, review it briefly before starting to prepare performance discussions. This will help to assure that performance checks or evaluations are handled properly and on time.

Tips for Discussing Performance

Conducting an effective performance discussion takes some time and thought. Here are some suggestions to aid the team leader supervisor to prepare for a constructive performance feedback discussion.

Consider the relevant measurement period. Avoid the tendency to be swayed by performance events that occurred in the last month. While these recent events may seem fresher in memory, make an effort to think back over the full rating period. For example, if the rating period is quarterly, your rating should reflect earlier performance as well as recent events.

Use objective work data as much as possible, citing such data as examples of performance achievements or shortcomings that need attention and improvement. See the list above.

Distinguish between the levels of performance on different performance issues. Identify the strengths and weaknesses of the individual. Give credit where deserved, and offer suggestions for improvement when warranted. Employees have strengths and weaknesses in different areas, so it is highly unlikely that every performance measure will be exceeded.

Check any performance ratings guidelines or definitions if defined by your organization. One of the biggest employee complaints about performance discussions is the inconsistency of ratings between supervisors. Some team leaders or supervisors earn a reputation of being tough raters while others are viewed as "easy" raters. Greater consistency among supervisors in preparing performance ratings builds credibility for supervisors and the performance management process. A sample performance rating definition is included in the Appendix of this book.

Compare the individual's performance to a norm or performance standard, rather than the performance of other individual employees. The performance norm can be specified work requirements or it can be an informal average output which is typical for a proficient worker in that position.

Check any defined goals or objectives which were discussed with the employee at the start of the rating period. Note whether goals were achieved. If the goal was not achieved, note extenuating circumstances, if any, and be prepared to discuss the matter further with the employee.

Check the prior performance discussions or evaluations to compare if performance has improved, declined, or stayed the same. If performance deficiencies have been corrected from a prior evaluation, then it is important to record the performance improvement. However, if performance deficiencies have continued from a prior performance discussion, then stronger corrective action is needed.

Be accurate and objective in your performance ratings. Rate poor performance as well as good performance. A failure by the supervisor to identify poor performance allows the problem to continue. The obvious problem is that the employee is not made aware of the performance deficiency and therefore cannot correct it. Secondly, failure to document poor performance can create a liability for the employer in legal claims of discrimination or wrongful discharge.

Illustrative Case Example
"Repairing the Damage of Poor Service"

The owner of an equipment repair service found that he was losing business to competitors. Employees were unkempt and rude to customers. Inefficient work habits of technicians created repair delays resulting in customer complaints and loss of service contracts.

Because of service contract cancellations and falling profits, the service manager was under the gun to improve service. He looked at performance evaluation forms from several other firms in the area, but none seemed appropriate for service-oriented repair business.

Ultimately, he retained a human resources consultant who developed a performance rating system keyed to the meticulous service records which he maintained. A customer feedback system was implemented. Upon rendering service to the customer, the feedback reports were reviewed. Also, each order was analyzed to compare costs, material, and labor hours, compared to goals for efficiency and profitability.

The objectivity of the data aided in constructive performance discussions between the service manager and technicians. Soon, the efficiency of service calls improved, a dress code was enforced, and the firm began to win back lost service contracts.

***

Summary

The performance management process really begins at the time of hire, with a proper orientation of new employees. Daily performance feedback is essential to deal with errors, recognize achievements, and let employees know where they stand. Frequent, timely performance discussions are essential to maintain the credibility of your performance management process. In situations of misconduct, these issues should be discussed and documented on disciplinary warnings that are issued to the employee. When preparing for a performance discussion, refer to job records to assure objectivity.

Frankly Speaking

Make Performance Discussions Meaningful

Making performance discussions meaningful is a difficult task for many team leaders or supervisors. Unfortunately, some team leaders of supervisors just go through the motions with only a cursory comment to the employee about job performance at raise time. As a result, there is little real communication about the employee's job performance. The reasons for this are many and varied. Some supervisors are fearful of confrontation or dislike the performance management process because it is viewed as criticizing a subordinate.

The key to a meaningful performance discussion is preparation. A good performance discussion is a frank discussion between employee and supervisor in which the employee receives feedback on job performance, achievements are recognized, and suggestions for improvement are offered. A supervisor who has prepared for the discussion has an effective road map to guide his or her discussion with the employee. Preparation for a performance discussion should include checking goals and review of objective performance data. Once the discussion is completed, take care to document the discussion in the manner defined by your firm's performance management policy.

Twenty Tips for Productive Performance Discussions

1. Be Prepared - Take some time to be thorough in preparing for the performance discussion. By collecting this data before beginning, the team leader or supervisor can readily cite specific work examples to praise, critique, or clarify the feedback. Careful preparation will promote a more meaningful performance discussion.

2. Plan Your Discussion - Carefully plan your discussion with the employee. Many supervisors use the performance appraisal form as an outline to guide the discussion. Try to anticipate the employee's reaction to your performance ratings. Consider how you will respond to the employee's reaction. If you properly provided daily performance feedback during the rating period, there should be no surprises. Rather, the performance discussion will be a review of issues already discussed with the employee.

3. Get Approvals - Be sure that you have any required approvals from upper management or the firm's human resources department. It is a customary practice at many firms to require that performance appraisals and any pay adjustments be approved by upper management prior to a discussion with the employee.

4. Notify Employee - Notify the employee in advance regarding the performance discussion. Many firms schedule performance discussions quarterly or at other intervals. With the calendar features now part of E-mail or other messaging systems, you can easily notify the employee in advance, promoting more open and positive communications. The advance notice lets the employee know that you are prepared to discuss performance issues on a timely basis.

5. Collect Work Samples - Collect any facts, documents, reports, work samples, or other similar items which reflect the employee's job output. These samples will be useful to illustrate the employee's performance, promote objective evaluation of performance, and help to justify performance ratings. The use of work samples focuses the discussion on specific job output issues. Constructive suggestions on how to perform tasks more efficiently help to minimize emotional confrontations.

6. Allow Adequate Time - To have a meaningful discussion, be sure to allow adequate time to discuss job expectations and the employee's performance. As a general guide, performance feedback checks could be adequately covered in 15 - 20 minutes. Performance discussions with employees in more complex jobs such as skilled, administrative, professional, sales, or management positions maybe 30 minutes to an hour or more. The key factor is to allow sufficient time to discuss job requirements, rate the employee's performance, suggest ways to improve and to elicit employee response.

7. Avoid Interruptions - Pick an interview time and place where interruptions will be minimized or avoided. A private office, conference room, lunchroom (avoiding break or lunch periods) or other areas away from the main flow of work, are possible locations for performance discussions. It is disconcerting to have other employees walking by or coming into an office during a performance discussion. Telephone calls also disrupt the performance discussion. Turn cell phones off. Make an effort to prevent or avoid these interruptions.

8. Describe the Process - Experienced interviewers describe the purpose, process, and result of an interview to the interviewee. This technique is equally effective in a performance management and in informal feedback sessions as well. By telling the employee what will happen during the performance discussion, you reduce the employee's uncertainty and answer some of his or her questions. Secondly, it helps you to take charge of the discussion by defining what issues will be discussed.

9. Be Friendly Yet Businesslike - The tone of the performance discussion should be friendly, positive and businesslike. Avoid joking or nervous laughter during the discussion. Try to encourage the employee to relax. If the employee has serious or continuing performance problems, the supervisor's manner should be firm to convey the seriousness of the employee's poor performance.

10. Keep on Track - Keep to the subject at hand. Do not let the discussion wander into unrelated areas. Thorough preparation will help the supervisor to discuss specific performance issues and minimize unrelated discussions.

11. Follow performance management guidelines - One easy way to set a direction to the discussion is to follow the firm's performance management instruction or guideline. First, identify the performance goal, then the desired performance norm, and then your feedback on the employee's performance. When you compare the results of the employee's work to the expected norm, issues can be discussed on a more objective basis. Avoid personal criticisms or insulting remarks.

12. Praise Achievements - Recognition and praise for achievements is an important part of the performance management process. Giving credit, when due, helps the employee to know his or her efforts are recognized. Recognition is an effective motivator.

13. Identify Deficiencies - Identify performance deficiencies. Poor performance must be documented consistent with the firm's performance management policy guideline, and then discussed with the employee. Do not "beat around the bush" with vague generalities. Give specific examples of performance problems and then identify the desired level of performance. The employee will assume that performance is satisfactory unless the problems are specifically identified.

14. Sandwich Technique - A technique called the sandwich technique can be helpful when discussing performance problems. With this technique, the team leader or supervisor first compliments the employee on an aspect of good performance, then identifies a performance deficiency, and then follows up with another comment about good performance. Clearly, this technique softens the effect of discussing poor performance. Avoid overusing this technique. In cases of serious or repeated poor performance, be sure to describe the problem specifically and specify the desired performance.

15. Maintain Professionalism - The performance discussion should be constructive - not confrontational; pleasant and professional - not a contest of personalities; with an element of empathy rather than pitched emotion. Focus on job tasks, results, and accomplishments. Personal attacks upon the individual are likely to arouse an argumentative response or result in barriers to communication.

16. Offer Improvement Suggestions - Offer specific suggestions on how to improve performance, particularly when identifying performance problems. Performance improvement is not likely to occur merely by identifying the employee's mistakes. However, performance improvement is more likely when the employee understands proper work techniques and expected performance goals.

17. Set Performance Goals - One key to improved performance is setting performance goals. By defining performance goals, the employee has a target to work towards. To be effective, goal setting should include employee input. Goals should be achievable with some extra effort. Defined goals provide a basis to evaluate performance in the next rating period.

Performance coaching or feedback is a one on one discussion.

18. Discuss Performance, Then Pay - Many firms conduct performance discussions and pay adjustment discussions together. If this is the practice at your firm, then it is best to discuss performance first, and then explain how the performance rating has influenced the pay adjustment.

19. Don't Discredit the Company - Occasionally, an inexperienced team leader or supervisor may promise a pay raise or tell the employee that a recommended pay raise was cut by management. When a team leader or supervisor discredits the company in this fashion, this action really reflects poorly on the rater. Do not fall into this trap.

20. Encourage Employee Comments - A primary objective of the performance discussion is communication between employee and team leader or supervisor. Accordingly, encourage your employees to react to performance feedback. The employee may agree, disagree, or offer reasons (sometimes excuses) for performance problems. Listen to and consider the employee's comments.

Employee Signature

Traditional performance evaluation processes have a space for employee signature or e-signature. Employers using a performance management software, the application likely will have a provision for the employee and the team leader or supervisor to apply an electronic signature to document the completion of the performance or coaching discussion. This is usually done at the end of the performance discussion. The employee's written or electronic signature serves to acknowledge that the performance discussion occurred. Also, many performance management processes include a segment for employee comments. In the interest of constructive communication, invite the employee to make written comments which can be entered into the performance record.

In the event that the employee disagrees with any aspect of the performance discussion, encourage the employee to enter or write his or her side of the story in the space provided.

On occasion, an employee may disagree with performance ratings so strongly that he or she refuses to sign the appraisal form. In such cases, encourage the employee to write his or her feelings as described above. If the employee still adamantly refuses to sign the form, then invite another team leader or supervisor into your discussion to witness that the performance discussion occurred. The second supervisor can then attest that the performance discussion occurred and the employee refused to sign the performance document.

Employee Self-Ratings

Employee self-ratings is a technique used by some firms to promote greater employee participation in the performance management process. With the practice of employee self - ratings, the employee asked to evaluate his or her own performance. The supervisor also prepares a performance evaluation of the employee. Then team leader or supervisor and employee discuss and compare ratings. The goal is to achieve a consensus on the employee's performance. In the event of a disagreement, the supervisor's rating is the official rating. The employee self-rating technique may not be suited for every organization. For this technique to be effective, the supervisor must have a high degree of self-confidence and be comfortable with discussing performance issues with employees. Some firms have used the employee self-rating process on a one-time basis to introduce a new or revised performance management process to employees.

360 Degree Ratings

360-degree ratings are a performance management process that elicits performance feedback from various individuals in an organization who interact frequently or regularly with the employee in the course of performing job duties. Typically, a 360-rating process elicits performance evaluation information from peers, subordinates as well as one or more superiors who have occasion to observe the performance results of the individual being rated.

Many of the basic elements of the performance management process apply to the 360-rating process. This may include elements such as clarifying job responsibilities, defining measurable performance goals, and providing objective feedback of performance results. Since the 360-peer rating "street runs both ways," such feedback, of course, should be honest, constructive, job-related and tactfully communicated.

Career Planning

Since successful performance is essential to achieve career growth, the performance discussion provides an excellent opportunity to discuss the employee's career interests.

The degree of career planning discussions will vary with the organization and its human resource philosophies. Career planning will play a greater role in larger organizations with more promotional opportunities and in organizations that tend to promote from within.

Smaller firms, however, should not overlook the benefits of career planning discussions with employees. In smaller firms, workers tend to perform a wider variety of tasks. Because of this, job responsibilities may be adapted to coincide with individual career interests. Matching of employee interests with job duties promotes greater job satisfaction and lessens the likelihood of unwanted turnover. A career planning process typically includes the following steps:

+ The performance management process is an essential first step to identify performance strengths and weaknesses in the present position.

+ After discussing performance, elicit employee job or career interests. A supervisor should not be offended if an employee expresses interest in his or her job. An ambitious employee is more likely to accept greater responsibility and learn new tasks. Further, you enhance your own promotability by having a back-up who can fill in if you are promoted.

+ Develop a realistic career development plan with the employee. The plan should recognize the employee's interests, abilities, reasonable job progression, and available resources to aid the employee in further development.

+ Among the alternatives for career development, consider one or more of the following:
    - new job assignments
    - special projects
    - fill in or back-up responsibilities
    - on the job training
    - on-line training
    - continuing education
    - vendor training or workshops
    - workshops or seminars

+ Periodically review the employee's progress. Provide new job assignments or promotional opportunities as openings become available and the employee demonstrates sufficient capability.

Illustrative Case Example
"Communication Firm Fails to Communicate on Performance"

A communication equipment company experienced problems in dealing with employee performance at its various facilities. Managers discovered that a lack of performance rating guidelines had prompted each branch manager to adopt their own approach to correcting performance problems and handling performance discussions. The manager at one branch devised her own performance checklist and freely gave high ratings to justify pay raises for favored branch employees. Another branch manager developed a "Simon Legree" reputation because he was quick to discipline or discharge an employee for a performance problem. At a third branch, sales began to erode because the manager was ineffective in correcting customer service and order processing errors.

To resolve these problems, a human resource specialist met with managers to define relevant performance factors and develop an appropriate performance management process with policy guidelines for managers. The new performance system was introduced at a management training seminar. Company managers actively participated in training sessions which included a rating of employees in fictional case examples and role-play discussions to gain practical experience in the performance management process.

After a year of working with the performance management system, managers lauded the new system as an effective aid to dealing with performance issues, citing the following examples:

- Employee morale and customer service levels improved at all branches as a result of uniform performance check which eliminated favoritism.

- The company successfully defended a discrimination charge by showing objective performance ratings of poor performance which justified the individual's discharge.

- Unwanted turnover and transfers were reduced because the performance management system helped the branch managers to more openly discuss performance issues and resolve problems.

***

Summary

Some team leaders or supervisors just go through the motions with only cursory comments about performance at raise time. Primary causes for this short-coming are lack of guidelines, lack of preparation, and lack of training.

The performance discussion with the employee is really the heart of the performance management process. Planning and preparation are important. Conduct the discussion in a private area without interruptions. Use a friendly yet business-like manner that focuses on specific job performance issues using the appraisal form to guide the discussion. Praise or critique performance, offering suggestions for improvement. Encourage open communication and discussion.

Money Matters

An Overview of Factors That Influence Pay

There are a variety of factors that influence how employers determine what to pay their employees. A very brief overview is provided here to help team leaders and supervisors better understand how pay is administered. Federal and state laws define requirements for overtime pay for certain covered employees while other categories of employees are deemed to be exempt from overtime pay. State laws in certain areas specify minimum wage levels, and frequency of pay periods and timeliness of issues pay to employees. Where there are union agreements covering certain groups of employees, the union agreement specifies details relating to pay and benefits. Other factors that influence how an employer sets pay include the firm's industry, its geographic location, the firm's profitability, and competitive salary trends.

Additional factors can influence how an employer administers pay for particular employees. Such factors can include job responsibility, education and qualifications, tenure or length of service and job performance. In the current job market, which is considered to be close to full employment, there is a high degree of competition for employees with certain skills and abilities working in high demand jobs, sometimes referred to as "hot skills jobs." According to a PayScale 2019 Best Practices report, 50% of participating employers reported that employee performance was a key determinant in setting and adjusting employee pay. Other significant factors cited were retention of individuals with valued skills, maintaining fair internal pay equity, and tenure.[31]

According to the Mercer 2018/2019 Compensation Survey, 80% of 1500 reporting firms evaluate and update salary increase budgets to remain competitive. The Mercer survey also reported that 77% of firms consider competitive practices when rewarding individual employee performance. The Mercer survey also reported that 78% of firms cite concerns about the retention of employees and 73% have concerns about setting pay rates in order to attract employees with needed skills and experience.[32]

Pay for Performance

A majority of employers believe in the idea of pay for performance. According to the World and Work 2017 Inventory of Total Rewards Programs & Practices, 94% of responding employers report that performance-based pay increases or merit increases are used for some or all of their employees. The frequency performance-based pay was somewhat less at health care and social assistance entities which reported the use of such practice at 87%. The frequency of performance-based pay in reporting Public sector employers was 71%.[33]

The Mercer survey cited above bears out comparable findings reporting that 88% of organizations still use individual performance to drive base salary adjustments.[34]

The PayScale survey of best practices, cited previously, further reported that the most typical form of variable pay used to reward performance was the individual incentive bonus, reported by 66%of companies and that the overwhelming basis of payout on incentive plans was an annual bonus.[35]

In preparing this publication, we recognize that team leaders and supervisors must administer employee compensation according to the guidelines and instructions of their employer. Larger firms are more likely to define guidelines or policies relating to the administration of employee compensation, while smaller and growing firms are often likely to use a high degree of management discretion in setting pay and deciding how pay adjustments are granted. Within this context, in this section, we provide useful tips to help team leaders and supervisors better correlate pay for performance where the employer's policy or practice permits their input.

Is Pay a Motivator?

Is pay a motivator for employees? Industrial psychologists have debated this issue for years. Most supervisors will agree that employee perception of pay is a factor that affects turnover, absences, morale, and motivation. For this reason, it is important for supervisors and managers to effectively communicate pay information. The performance management process provides an ideal medium for the supervisor to discuss the employee's performance and its influence on pay rates or pay adjustments.

The basic elements of motivation include the following:

a) an individual's desire or need.

b) an effort to meet the desire or need.

c) attainment of the desire or need.

In an employment setting, various factors can serve as motivators for employees. Among the motivators are pay, recognition, advancement, power, time off work, and other rewards. The performance management process provides an opportunity for the supervisor to identify the employee's motivators. Several examples are offered.

PAY - For the employee who is motivated by pay, the team leader or supervisor can set performance goals and then reward the employee with a pay increase for the attainment of the goals. Conversely, failure to attain the goals or poor performance should result in a lower or delayed pay increase or even denial of a pay increase.

RECOGNITION - For the employee who seeks recognition, performance discussions help to meet this need. During the performance appraisal discussion, the supervisor can recognize and compliment the employee for work achievements. For many individuals, recognition from the boss is important. Appreciation of the employee's efforts will contribute to continued efforts and motivation by the employee.

ADVANCEMENT - The performance discussion provides for management an opportunity to evaluate the employee for advancement. Prior performance records provide a documented resource of information on the individual's job performance to aid in considering him or her for promotion. Further, after discussing current performance issues, the team leader or supervisor can explore the employee's interests in career advancement and develop action plans or job assignments that will prepare the employee for promotion.

OTHER REWARDS - The performance management process can serve as a basis to provide various rewards to deserving employees. Performance incentives, bonuses, or other kinds of non-financial incentives as allowed by the employer can be provided based upon a team leader or supervisor's performance evaluations as well as other eligibility criteria established by management or compensation specialists.

New Rewards

Leading organizations that are breaking from old pay for performance traditions are also new ground in finding new ways to reward employees according to the 2018 Deloitte Global Human Capital Trends report. The emerging trend is towards creating holistic rewards systems that are more personalized and agile in order to attract, motivate and develop talent. The firms at the forefront of this transition are developing rewards that are delivered more continuously and that are more closely aligned with individual preferences and considering the employees' role and contribution to the organization.

Examples of individualized rewards may include identifying and offering rewards that cater to employee's lives inside and outside of work, including new kinds of paid days off or tailored benefits. Yet, even as these winds of change reflect new directions where 76 percent of respondents report re-invigorating performance management practices, the Deloitte report further acknowledges that 91 percent of companies still follow the customary practice of conducting salary review once a year.[36]

Separating Pay and Performance Discussions

"It's time for your review." This simple statement means different things to different people. The team leader or supervisor who says this to the employee may be referring to a periodic or annual performance discussion. The employee, on the other hand, is thinking, "It's time for my pay raise." In spite of the best efforts of team leaders, supervisors, and human resource professionals, this misunderstanding is commonplace at many firms. In many firms, the pay adjustments and performance discussions occur simultaneously or closely correlated. Secondly, most firms grant pay raises at least annually. For these reasons, it is understandable that employees consider the "review" to be a pay increase.

Steffen Maier, co-founder of Impraiser, writing in Entrepreneur, suggests that firms keep one annual review for compensation decisions. He notes that the most commonly used method of performance management is to introduce more continuous informal feedback and quarterly performance reviews, but continue to keep one annual review specifically for making compensation decisions. Rather than being in the dark until the annual review, employees will know where they are and how they've improved at each quarterly check-in. Compensation is still linked to end of the year feedback but the feedback they receive throughout the year is focused on growth and development.[37]

Team leaders and supervisors can do several things to place the proper emphasis on the performance aspects of a performance discussion.

+ Use the term that actually described your firm's performance management process. If the performance management process is described as a "coaching discussion," or a "review of goal achievement," or "a rating," or an "appraisal" or "evaluation," describe the discussion by the appropriate term instead of referring to "your review."

+ Explain the difference between a pay adjustment and a performance discussion when orientating new employees.

+ When scheduling performance discussions, advise employees whether the discussion will cover performance, pay, or both.

+ At the start of the performance discussion, explain to the employee whether the discussion will cover performance, pay, or both.

+ Explain that a performance discussion may occur without a pay adjustment.

+ Explain that the employee's performance must be satisfactory in order to be considered for a pay adjustment.

+ Explain that poor performance is sufficient grounds to delay or deny a pay increase.

+ Explain further that poor performance may be sufficient grounds for discharge.

Anticipate employee questions and be prepared with a response.

Some firms have elected to separate the pay discussion from the performance discussion. The separate discussions may occur a day, week or even a month apart. With separate discussions, the employee's performance is covered first, and the pay change discussed subsequently. With this procedure, the key benefit is that you have the employee's undivided attention to the performance issues. The drawback, of course, is that the approach requires two separate discussions with each employee. For some supervisors, this may be too time-consuming.

Checklist for Supervisors - Tips on Discussing Pay

+ Learn your organization's pay philosophy. Discuss your organization's pay philosophy with your superior or the Human Resources Specialist. Does your firm try to be a pay leader or match competitive rates in the area? Are benefits viewed as an important part of the total compensation for employees? You can discuss pay issues more confidently with employees when you have a better understanding of your firm's pay philosophy.

+ Be sure that you understand and follow the performance management and pay review procedures in your organization. If there are written management procedures, review these prior to discussing pay issues with employees.

+ Avoid promising a specific pay rate, raise, or effective date until this information has been approved by management. If you make a promise that is later turned down by superiors, this reflects poorly on your credibility as a team leader or supervisor.

+ Obtain necessary approvals prior to discussing a specific pay rate or pay adjustment with an employee.

+ Protect the confidentiality of pay issues. Exercise caution to avoid the release of payroll records or information. Pay information is a confidential matter between the supervisor and the employee. Do not discuss or compare an employee's pay to another.

+ Discuss the relationship between pay and performance. It is permissible to explain how performance ratings influence the pay rate or pay adjustment. Be sure to follow your firm's policies about salary plan confidentiality and not disclosing detail of pay levels of pay ranges unless such practice is permitted.

+ Be specific to identify an employee's performance problems when poor performance is a basis to deny, reduce, or delay a pay adjustment.

+ Discuss pay in private. Respect the employee's concern for confidentiality by discussing pay issues in a private office or area where the discussion will not be overheard by others.

+ Anticipate employee questions about pay and be prepared with responses. You can discuss pay issues clearly and confidently when you understand your firm's pay philosophy and pay administration practices.

+ Avoid discrediting management or blaming superiors if you are called upon to communicate a pay raise which is lower than requested or expected. Such negative comments only reflect poorly on yourself and tend to cause poor morale.

+ Be prepared to "sell" the pay package. As a member of management, it is your responsibility to represent pay issues to employees in a way that emphasizes the positive aspects of employment with your firm.

+ Discuss performance issues first when your firm's practice requires a combined pay and performance discussion. This way, you can explain how the employee's performance influenced the pay adjustment.

+ Explain the big picture. Explain how business conditions, the economy, sales, etc. influence the organization's income or profits and the ability to provide pay increases for employees.

+ Explain the firm's total compensation program including insurances, paid absences, government-required benefits, etc. For many firms, benefits are a significant cost which represents 30% to 35% of the total compensation program.

+ Respond to employee questions as honestly as possible without violating confidentiality guidelines.

+ Be on time when scheduling performance discussions and processing pay adjustments. A timely pay review is very important to the employee. Your lateness or inattention to the matter can contribute to lower morale or performance problems.

There's No Raise This Year

One of the toughest tasks faced by a team leader or supervisor is discussing pay during periods of economic restraint. These are the tough times when pay adjustments are smaller, delayed or withheld. During periods of prosperity, employees become accustomed to annual salary increases. Unfortunately, when business or budgetary conditions become tight, it is usually the supervisor's responsibility to deliver the bad news about pay to employees.

The decision to delay, reduce, or withhold general pay adjustments is normally made by top management. Here are some tips for supervisors:

+ Confer with superiors to gain a thorough understanding of the business conditions which lead to the decision to suspend or reduce pay increases. An understanding of this big picture helps to put the pay issue into a proper perspective.

+ Identify other cost control measures that are being undertaken. Let your employees know that management has taken other cost reduction steps prior to or simultaneously with the pay limits. Reduction of hours, curtailment of overtime, not filling job vacancies, are examples of effective cost-cutting techniques.

+ Explain to the employee how business conditions have reduced pay adjustments. Also, explain how individual performance issues have affected pay increases.

+ Emphasize the positive aspects of the employment relationship such as company-paid benefits, working conditions, location, and other similar benefits or rewards of continued employment with your firm.

+ Emphasize the need for teamwork, cooperation, and continued efforts by all employees in order to get through the tough times.

+ Show empathy and understanding when discussing pay limitations. Most likely, other employees including yourself are similarly affected by a pay freeze or a reduction in the amount of a pay increase.

+ Avoid making promises of future pay increases or commitments about job security. Such promises, if unfulfilled will further erode morale. Comments about job security should be avoided because such statements could be viewed as binding commitments resulting in an adverse judgment against the firm in a wrongful discharge lawsuit.

Remember: Careful preparation in the discussion of pay issues is important to prevent or minimize misunderstandings about pay.

Illustrative Case Example
"Penny Wise and Pound Foolish"

A graphic arts company in a metropolitan area had a large number of unskilled and semi-skilled workers. Company management had elected to set starting wages and pay rates at lower than average levels compared to the surrounding area. Management reasoned that because of the ready availability of the labor force in the area, a lower pay rate was acceptable. However, over a period of time, this practice contributed to excessive turnover, employee discontent, marginal quality from inexperienced workers, and recruiting and training costs.

Ultimately, the company undertook a pay study and formulated a plan to raise wages to competitive levels. Pay practices were revised to better correlate pay adjustments to performance ratings. Supervisors received training and guidelines on how to discuss pay issues with employees. Typical employee questions were identified and management drafted suggestion responses to aid supervisors in fielding pay questions. Within three months of implementation of the new pay policies, turnover was cut in half and recruiting costs dropped 60%.

Management observed improved quality and better morale as employees worked harder for better performance ratings and pay adjustments.

***

Summary

Employee perception of pay is a factor that affects turnover, absences, morale, and motivation. For these reasons, team leaders or supervisors must effectively communicate pay information. The performance management process provides a medium to correlate performance and pay, provide recognition, evaluate workers for advancement, and provide other rewards. Some firms elect to separate performance and pay discussions in order to achieve a maximum emphasis on each issue.

Employees often perceive scheduled performance discussions as a pay review. Team leaders and supervisors need to clearly communicate the distinction between performance discussions and pay adjustment discussions. When discussing pay, learn your firm's philosophy and follow policy guidelines. Protect pay confidentiality, avoid promises, and be prepared to "sell" pay issues by explaining the full compensation package. Focus on performance issues first when discussing performance and pay at the same time.

A Bad Apple in the Bunch

Problem Solving with Performance Check-ins

As described earlier in this book, one of the growing trends is to use more frequent informal performance check-is rather than the traditional performance appraisal process. This approach certainly provides a basis for the team leader or supervisor to have immediate feedback discussions that recognize good performance and identify any performance concerns. In the event that there are performance problems or behavioral misconduct, such matters should be covered during the check-in discussion. It is an opportunity to correct the behavior that, if left unchecked could grow worse. The suggestions that follow can help the team leader or supervisor to deal with a poorly performing employee and correct a problem avoiding an uncomfortable discharge discussion.

Confronting Poor Performance

One issue that every team leader or supervisor must face is confronting the poor performance of a team member or a subordinate. Unfortunately, too many team members or supervisors allow an individual's performance problem to continue uncorrected for too long before dealing with the issue. Perhaps, during the early stages of the problem, the team leader or supervisor tries to be understanding and allows the problem to continue hoping that the employee will resolve the matter. However, as problems continue to mount, the one in charge sometimes loses patience and then abruptly explodes in anger or possibly fires the errant employee. Such a course of action eliminates the performance problem, but in today's litigious society, it also may contribute to a wrongful discharge lawsuit by the former employee.

Poor performance does not just go away. On the contrary, it is more likely to continue and worsen unless corrective action is taken by the team leader or supervisor. Unless properly trained and advised of errors, the employee likely assumes that work performance is okay. The supervisor has a responsibility to confront the performance problems.

Dealing with Misconduct

Employee misconduct can generally be defined as employee actions or behavior which violates published rules or policy, customary workplace practices, or generally accepted norms of behavior in a working environment. Common examples of misconduct may include theft, insubordination, use of drugs or alcohol on the job, falsification of records, or excessive absenteeism.

Most firms define disciplinary rules for employees. These rules are typically enforced through progressive disciplinary procedures. Progressive discipline commonly includes increasingly severe actions for repeated, subsequent, or serious violations of disciplinary rules. Disciplinary actions commonly take the form of verbal warnings, written warnings, suspension without pay and ultimately discharge. Disciplinary warnings normally focus on a specific incident of misconduct. Disciplinary warnings are one tool to help the supervisor deal with employee misconduct.

Misconduct must be addressed immediately. As soon as the team leader or supervisor is aware of the situation, corrective action should include the following:

1) investigate the incident.

2) Verify facts by checking records or getting statements of any witnesses.

3) Speak with the employee in private. Avoid a "public" reprimand. In a union environment, be sure to have the union steward present in any disciplinary discussion.

4) Report the issue to your superior or human resources if your firm's policy requires their involvement in discipline or other job actions.

5) Specify the nature of the misconduct and why it is inappropriate.

6) Specify what corrective action will be taken, i.e.: verbal warning, written warning, or another similar warning.

7) In cases of serious misconduct, suspension or discharge may be warranted. Immediate on-the-spot discharge is

discouraged. Rather, suspend the employee, verify the facts of the case, and confer with superiors and/or the human resource specialist to make sure that discharge is a proper action. Refer to and follow any policy guidelines published in your firm's policy manual or employee handbook. Your discharge action can be effective at the conclusion of the suspension period.

8) Document the warning as specified by your firm's discipline policy. Some firms use a warning statement or corrective action memo, with the employee receiving one copy and retain one copy for the human resources file.

9) In cases of subsequent or repeated misconduct, keep your superior or human resources informed. You may be instructed to take progressively more severe action.

10) Be alert for "red flags" that may indicate potential threatening or violent conduct by an employee who is being disciplined or discharged. Confer with human resources or security personnel when planning to conduct a sensitive discussion with a potentially troublesome employee.

Dealing with Performance Problems

An employee's job performance problems can be distinguished from misconduct. Where misconduct is typically deliberate inappropriate behavior, performance problems can be defined as employee action or inaction which causes work tasks to be performed poorly or in a manner that fails to meet expectations. Examples of poor performance may be errors in the preparation of data or reports, inefficient operation of equipment or machines, inability to complete tasks on time, or failure to meet standards for quantity or quality of work.

Performance problems may relate to one or more aspects of the work activity. When work problems come to the supervisor's attention, the first priority is to direct employees to take necessary action to correct or respond to the problem. Secondly, it is important that the team leader or supervisor discuss the problem with the employee noting the error and what should be done in the future to prevent or resolve the problem. Cite examples and give specific instructions to ensure that the employee will properly handle the situation in the future.

In the event the employee's performance continues to be below expectations, then further action is needed. If appropriate, arrange for or provide further training for the employee.

Adapt your style and approach for dealing with subsequent or repeated performance problems. In a manner similar to progressive discipline, subsequent performance discussions should be more direct noting the specific performance standards which must be met.

Develop a Performance Plan

A performance plan is an effective way to help an employee to overcome a performance problem. When one or two prior performance discussions fail to correct the problem a more detailed approach is necessary. Here are some suggestions for a performance plan:

+ Begin your plan by preparing a performance evaluation detailing goals and required performance level. In this evaluation, list the employee's responsibilities and identify performance strengths as well as weaknesses.

+ Identify specific tasks, activities, skills, etc., to be improved.

+ Define a performance standard or an expected level of performance which the employee must attain. Provide objective quantifiable performance guidelines as much as possible.

+ Specify a time period for further evaluation of the employee's efforts. The time period should be a reasonable period in which the employee's effort can fairly be measured and evaluated. Depending on the job and performance factors involved, such an evaluation period could be a week, month, or even a three- month period.

+ Make specific suggestions on how tasks can be performed better. Many jobs or tasks have certain shortcuts or techniques used by experienced employees. Pass along any suggestions to help the employee do a better job.

+ Consider and arrange participation for the employee in training, seminars, or workshops which are relevant to the employee's job. Such training may be on the job provided by supervisors or human resource/training specialists. In many areas, off-site educational programs are available through trade schools, community colleges or universities. Also, in many industries, professional associations provide training courses designed to help employees improve and upgrade skills or learn new job skills.

+ Discuss the performance plan with the employee. Seek to obtain the employee's agreement and commitment to achieve the specified performance requirements. Some "give and take" in the discussion of performance goals or evaluation time periods may be appropriate. However, the requirement for performance improvement to an acceptable level should not be a negotiable factor.

+ Conduct a follow-up performance discussion at the specified time intervals or time period. Recognize any performance improvements made by the employee. Identify any continued shortcomings and offer suggestions on how to improve.

+ Document the performance plan according to your firm's performance management policy. Obtain the employee's signature on the performance plan to record participation in this discussion.

+ Emphasize a positive tone throughout the performance discussions with constructive suggestions on how tasks can be performed better. Avoid personal criticisms.

Get a Second Opinion

Sometimes a team leader or supervisor can benefit from a second opinion when dealing with an employee's performance problems. The advice can come from your superior or human resource specialist. Your superior most likely has had prior experience in dealing with similar employee performance problems. He or she can offer advice on ways to work with the employee to obtain improved job performance.

Likewise, it can be helpful to confer with your organization's human resource specialists for ideas on working with a problem employee. The human resource specialist can provide advice on proper documentation of performance problems, suggested approaches for performance discussions, and promote consistency by outlining how other similar cases have been handled.

Probationary Period

An important aspect of correcting poor performance is making sure that the employee understands the severity of the problem. Too many times, unfortunately, a supervisor does not clearly explain the importance of correcting the performance problem. If the importance is not made clear, the employee does not realize that his or her job may be in jeopardy. As a result, the employee may not try as hard to correct the problem.

A probationary period is one way to emphasize the severity of the problem. It also puts the employee on notice to correct the performance problem or be subject to dismissal. A probationary period can coincide with the performance plan period explained earlier. The probationary period serves as a final warning to the employee.

A probationary period or final warning also helps to justify any resulting dismissal. It shows that the employee was given a final warning, an opportunity to correct performance problems and clearly lays the groundwork to support a dismissal if the employee's performance fails to improve. Such actions can be key to defending any claim, allegation, or lawsuit filed by a discharged former employee.

Document Corrective Actions

Every human resource specialist can relate a story of a dismissal situation in which there is no documentation to support management's contention of an employee's poor performance. In such cases, there is usually a history of performance problems, but for various reasons, the supervisor has allowed the problem to continue. Finally, a serious incident occurs, prompting the supervisor to fire the employee. A check of the personnel file reveals a history of pay increases, few if any disciplinary warnings, and neutral or even positive performance ratings. These are also likely to be the cases that end up before an unemployment insurance hearing referee or a government equal opportunity claims investigator or a judge considering a wrongful discharge lawsuit. Such cases can result in significant legal liability for the firm.

A supervisor can help to reduce the firm's liability by documenting employee performance records such as performance discussions or evaluations, disciplinary warnings, final warning notices, and any performance plans. The recommended process is this: 1) keep your superior and the human resources specialist aware of pending problem performance, 2) take appropriate corrective action, 3) record the corrective action in a performance document or system, 4) obtain employee's signature and provide a copy to the employee, 5) keep your superior and the human resources specialist aware of corrective action taken. These records will help justify a dismissal and can be a ready defense if a case goes to court or a government hearing.

What if the employee complains about performance ratings?

Every team leader or supervisor, likely has had an employee complain that a low-performance rating is unfair. This may occur when you have given an employee a lower performance rating than he or she may have received previously, or when the employee may have received higher performance ratings in the past from another supervisor. Many performance management plans include a procedure for the employee to provide a response or reply to the performance rating if he or she disagrees with the rating.

Ask the employee to identify what their specific concerns may be. You can also ask why the employee feels that the evaluation may be unfair. Begin by getting information, as specific as possible, from the employee without initially responding or trying to justify your rating. Once you have a better or full understanding of the issues, you can respond calmly and objectively. If, for example, there were clearly defined performance objectives and the employee failed to meet the objective, this information can be reviewed with the employee.

Ensure that employees are not held to higher standards or given negative evaluations because of factors that are defined as protected class categories under state or federal anti-bias laws. These can include basis such as race, color, religion, sex (including pregnancy, sexual orientation, or gender identity), national origin, disability, age (40 or older), genetic information (including family medical history). Also, see the section entitled "Handling Internal Discrimination Complaints about Performance Evaluations."

Illustrative Case Example
"Customer Reject Prompts Performance Plan"

A growing internet apparel firm was experiencing problems in maintaining product quality. Customer complaints were increasing and credits on returned goods were cutting into profits. Finally, the inevitable occurred. A prominent customer returned a big order and refused to pay for the poor-quality merchandise.

To prevent a recurrence of a similar problem, the company president instituted numerous changes. One of the corrective actions taken was the development of a performance improvement plan rather than the discharge of the production manager. This plan identified specific performance measures, goals, and timetables. The plan defined specific guidelines for productivity, quality levels, reduction of waste, control of labor costs, and accountability to accomplish these goals over a six-month period.

As a result of this plan, the firm implemented improved product inspection checks, quality assurance guidelines, and training for employees and supervisors. Through improved quality, the company again won the business of the major customer by year-end.

***

Summary

One important supervisory responsibility is confronting and correcting poor performance. Misconduct typically should be dealt with through disciplinary warnings. Poor performance typically is dealt with through performance discussions. A performance plan is an effective way to help an employee overcome a performance problem. The performance plan identifies strengths and weaknesses and then defines specific performance goals, with a completion timetable for the employee. In cases of serious performance problems, the employee can be given a final warning and put on a probationary status. It is recommended that the supervisor confers with a superior or human resources specialist for advice on dealing with performance problems. Be sure to document corrective actions by using disciplinary warnings or a counseling record.

Performance Management and The Law

Performance Appraisals Subject to Labor Laws

Supervisors and managers make employment decisions daily on matters such as hiring, pay, promotions, job assignments, appraising performance, discipline, or discharge. Performance management, like all other employment decisions, is subject to State and Federal labor laws and regulations.

Performance management processes are often the key basis for pay adjustments, bonus compensation, promotions, transfers or discharges. Improper or discriminatory employment decisions can create a liability for your organization. For these reasons, it is important for supervisors to have an understanding of performance management and the law.

Preventing Discrimination

Performance appraisals must be administered in a fair and consistent manner which avoids discrimination. Discriminatory performance ratings or other use of performance management processes to adversely affect the employment of minorities, females or other protected classes can violate equal employment opportunity laws. If disproportionately high numbers of minorities or females are excluded from promotions or given lower performance ratings or pay increases, the employer may be called upon to show that its performance management process is a valid measure of performance.

Protected class categories under Federal laws include the following bases: age, race, sex, religion, national origin, color, pregnancy, disability, genetic information, and retaliation for engaging in protected activity relating to any of the above basis categories. Additional protected categories may be defined by laws administered by state or city fair employment practice agencies (FEPA).

One of the standards used by the Equal Employment Opportunity Commission (EEOC) for judging the appropriateness of performance appraisals is defined in the Uniform Guidelines on Employee Selection Procedures (1978). The key guideline for supervisors and managers is to focus performance evaluations on an objective evaluation of job-related criteria.

An individual who believes that he or she has experienced employment discrimination may contact the EEOC or a FEPA to present a charge of discrimination against the employer. The agency will investigate the matter and ask for the employer's response. Based on the evidence presented by the parties, the agency may issue a Cause finding where there is reasonable cause to believe that discrimination occurred and seek to conciliate a resolution. In the event that there is insufficient evidence to prove a violation, the agency will issue a No Cause finding and a right to sue letter which gives the charging party an opportunity to pursue the matter in court within a specified time period. The courts will evaluate the matter based upon the law and the precedent in the jurisdiction.

Understanding Employment-At-Will

Years ago, when the United States was formed, our founders borrowing many legal concepts from England, including the concept of employment at will. This meant that workers could seek employment and quit at will, and likewise that the employer could hire workers when needed and lay off workers when the business slacked off. As our society and the workplace became more complicated, we saw lawsuits by former employees who alleged wrongful discharge. This area of law has grown significantly and now represents significant potential liabilities for employers. An emerging area of employment law, these cases are initiated in state courts by former employees who feel that they were discharged unfairly by their former employers. Common examples of wrongful discharge are summarized below:

+ Public-policy exceptions such as whistle-blowing or otherwise engaging in protected, concerted activities which the courts may deem a limitation to a company's ability to terminate at whim under the employment-at-will;

+ Statutory exceptions such as protected class bases like those outlined in Title VII of the Civil Rights Act of 1964, which prohibits discrimination on the basis of sex, race, color, religion, or national origin;

+ Employment contracts including individual agreements and collective bargaining agreements;

+ Implied contract exceptions or implied covenants of good faith and fair dealing such as potential promises made in employee handbooks.[38]

There are several areas where performance management can affect the discharge process. When an employee's poor performance results in a discharge, it is vitally important that the supervisor accurately document the performance problems according to the employer's performance management process. A critical performance evaluation can serve as a final warning to the employee while giving the employee an opportunity to correct the performance problems. In the event the employee's performance fails to improve, the supervisor then has a documented and justified basis to proceed with the discharge.

Another reason that accurate performance ratings are essential is that performance evaluation records and other employment documents become evidence in legal proceedings. Performance ratings that detail performance problems will support the discharge action in a court or hearing. On the other hand, an absence of critical performance evaluations or records reflecting good performance is likely to sway a judge or jury to side for the employee in a wrongful discharge case.

Be sure to follow policies published in an employee handbook or management policy manual, particularly when handling cases resulting in discharge. In many areas, state courts have held that policy information in a personnel policy manual may be contractually binding upon the employer. When a supervisor disregards a published policy while handling an employee separation, there is a greater likelihood of a finding of wrongful discharge.

Constructive Discharge

Constructive discharge occurs when an employer deliberately makes working conditions for an employee so intolerable that the employee is forced into voluntary resignation.

Team leaders and supervisors need to recognize that deliberate and unreasonable actions in dealing with employees may create a liability for their employer if the employee files a discrimination charge or wrongful discharge lawsuit.

For this reason, performance management processes should fairly document job-related performance, good and bad. Further, the administration of the performance appraisal should be consistent with other appraisals given to other employees for similar situations. Avoid the tendency to arbitrarily "build a case" against an employee, contrive a situation, create excessive documentation, or define unreasonable standards of performance. Such actions may be viewed as constructive discharge.

Reasonable Accommodation for Disabilities

The Americans with Disabilities Act of 1990 (ADA) prohibits discrimination against qualified disabled individuals in all employment practices, including performance appraisals. Also, other various state laws require nondiscrimination qualified disabled workers.

Under these laws, employers are required to make reasonable accommodation for qualified individuals with a disability. Examples of reasonable accommodations cited in the regulations include modifying work schedules, restructuring or reassigning jobs, or modifying or acquiring new equipment to aid the disabled worker. Accommodations are not required if the change will impose an undue hardship on the organization.

Based upon interpretive guidelines on disability discrimination, employers are not required to lower quality or quantity standards in order to make an accommodation for a disabled individual. A temporary "light duty" assignment normally would not affect a performance standard. However, if a job is restructured to accommodate a permanent limiting condition, the change may have an effect on performance standards. The disabled individual or any other incumbent can be held accountable to perform the job's essential functions and to meet reasonable job-related performance standards. The ADA recognizes a job description as the identification of a job's essential functions. Each accommodation request must be evaluated on a case by case basis and documentation of the evaluation is recommended.

Performance Management and Unions

Traditionally, formal performance management practices were seldom used in industrial and craft union environments. In craft union work, once the learner completed the apprenticeship, he or she was recognized as a journeyman, fully trained to perform the craft. Both craft and industrial, union contracts tend to emphasize seniority as a key criterion for promotions, pay progression, job assignments, and other conditions of employment.

More recently, however, unions have become more open to recognizing the benefits of performance-oriented work procedures. Declining union membership rolls, a growing diversity of unionism into "white collar" occupations including public sector and health care, and the manufacturing employer's need for improved productivity due to international competition are factors that prompt unions to more readily accept performance management processes as part of the employment relationship.

Performance management is an appropriate subject of bargaining. Therefore, a supervisor in a union environment should not unilaterally start a performance evaluation process without first discussing the matter with superiors and human resource specialists. In situations where the union contract defines a performance appraisal or merit system, the supervisor is responsible to administer the system according to the union agreement. Arbitrators generally have looked upon performance appraisal or merit rating plans as an aid in judging an employee's fitness and ability when interpreting contract clauses.

In one arbitration case example where the contract provided that seniority shall govern where ability, skill, and efficiency are substantially equal, the arbitrator held that management's institution of a performance appraisal plan was a suitable method to determine the relative ability of employees.

Many union agreements include provisions requiring "just cause" as a basis for discharge. The just cause requirement refers to a worker's failure to comply with the union agreement or misconduct in violation of safety or disciplinary rules. A worker's poor performance may also be considered just cause for dismissal. In reviewing discharge cases, arbitrators give credence to prior warnings in support of a discharge action. Where a firm has a performance appraisal procedure in place and uses it to fairly document performance problems that result in discharge, such actions will help support the management position presented to an arbitrator.

A properly conducted and documented performance management   process can support employment decisions in a legal claim.

Case Illustrations

The performance management process can play an integral role in defending a company's actions in a discrimination allegation or wrongful discharge lawsuit. However, both the evaluation system and its administration must be a fair measure of job-related performance. Otherwise, the firm is likely to incur the liability of a losing case. Various case examples are highlighted below:

Lack of Honest Evaluations Caused Discrimination

An employer's failure to evaluate a black employee honestly concerning job performance to avoid charges of race discrimination was viewed by the court as proof of race discrimination. While the supervisor had told the employee that

101

her productivity was low, management elected to let the performance problems continue without formal reprimand, even giving the employee a satisfactory performance review with a merit pay raise. She was later released for poor performance. In judging her discrimination claim, an appeals court held that by not criticizing her performance, the company had treated her differently, constituting discrimination.

Lack of Job-Related Criteria Creates Discriminatory Promotion Practice

A manufacturing company had followed a practice of relying solely on subjective supervisor recommendations when evaluating employees for promotions. In considering a discrimination complaint, the court found that the lack of written instructions pertaining to qualifications for promotion resulted in subjective discriminatory practices.

Performance Ratings Justify Discharge

A 60-year-old employee, laid off due to poor performance, filed on an age discrimination complaint against the employer. In responding to the claim, the employer produced documented evidence of prior performance ratings detailing the employee's poor performance and company efforts to resolve the problem. In deciding the case, the court agreed with the company's position that the poor performance justified the discharge.

Employer Duty: Use "Reasonable Care" to Fairly Communicate in Performance Appraisals

A 22-year employee with a record of adequate service was discharged for performance deficiencies. In deciding this case, the court asserted that the employer has a duty to use "reasonable care" in carrying out the performance evaluation process. The responsible standard is that of a reasonable person performing the performance review. The employer has a responsibility to warn the employee when poor performance may create a discharge possibility. Failure to provide such a warning may be viewed by the courts as employer negligence.

Subjective Performance Appraisal System Unfair

Ruling on a discharge case, the court found an employer's performance appraisal system unfair. Among the deficiencies in the appraisal system, the court cited the lack of a standard scoring system, lack of guidelines on weights of performance variables, and the allowance of supervisors to independently chose performance variables.

Performance Improvement Plan Rebuts Discrimination Claim

A minority sales representative claimed he was fired due to race discrimination. In its defense, the company stated that the individual was fired for poor performance and that he failed to respond to a performance improvement program. To support its case, the company presented evidence in which the performance improvement program identified specific deficiencies and set goals for improvement. The goals were specific with objective descriptions of improved selling techniques. The court agreed that the employee's failure to meet the goals constituted grounds for discharge.

Sexually Biased Ratings Judged Discriminatory

A male supervisor referred to a female subordinate as a "pushy broad" and gave her markedly lower ratings than her fellow male employees. An investigation of performance issues showed that her performance was comparable to others. The supervisor's biased performance ratings resulting in unfairly low evaluations of the female worker were judged to be a discriminatory practice.

A Pattern of Biased Ratings and Biased Remark Proved Discrimination

A 66-year-old employee experienced a culture of age discrimination where managers gave lower review scores to older workers and where the complaining employee was paid less than younger colleagues. When he was fired, 110 others shared his job title, but only the five fired were all over fifty years old. When he complained about his discharge, he was told that a senior manager felt they had been with the company for too long. He sued and was able to prove that because of his age, and for no other reason, he suffered discrimination.

Handling Internal Discrimination Complaints about Performance Evaluations

As a team leader or supervisor, conducting performance management discussion, you may receive a complaint from an employee that he or she felt that a performance discussion was unfair or discriminatory. This can readily occur when you have given an employee a lower performance rating than he or she may have received previously. It can also occur in situations where the employee may have received higher performance ratings in the past from another supervisor.

In such cases, since the complaint has been brought to your attention, you are in a position to discuss the matter further with the employee to identify what their specific concerns may be. You can also ask why the employee feels that the evaluation may be discriminatory. Begin by getting information, as specific as possible, from the employee without initially responding or trying to justify your rating. Once you have a better or full understanding of the issues, you can respond calmly and objectively. If, for example, there were clearly defined performance objectives and the employee failed to meet the objective, this information can be reviewed with the employee.[39]

An employee complaining about an unfair performance rating may make such a complaint because he or she believes that other employees performed equally or worse yet received better performance ratings or better pay increase. The team leader or supervisor would be expected to protect the confidentiality of pay and performance matters of other employees and to not discuss such matters with the complaining employee. It may be wise to inform your manager or the firm's human resources specialist that the employee has complained about his or her performance rating. The specialist may be able to offer some suggestions for responding to the complaint.

If, after a follow-up discussion, the employee is not satisfied with the outcome or if the complaint relates to how others were treated, the matter should be referred to your manager or to the Human Resources specialist. These individuals likely will conduct their own investigation or refer the matter to a human resources or legal specialist. The team leader or supervisor should not attempt in any way to prevent the concerned employee from presenting her or her complaint up the chain of command to the Human Resources representative, as such action could be viewed as retaliation for engaging in protected activity.

Keep Your Performance Management Process Legal - A Checklist for Team Leaders and Supervisors

+ Follow company procedures, guidelines, or applicable union agreements when administering the performance management process.

+ Focus performance evaluations on objective job-related criteria.

+ Examples of objective criteria deemed allowable by the courts include the quantity of work, quality of work, and completion of specific job-related goals.

+ Examples of vague or subjective criteria deemed inappropriate by the courts include adaptability, bearing, demeanor, manner, social behavior and subjective opinion of others.

+ Document performance problems accurately as defined by your performance management process or disciplinary warning procedure. Rate both good and bad performance characteristics. Permit the employee to receive a copy or have system access to the performance rating.

+ Obtain the employee's manual or electronic signature as allowed by your performance management system. The signature serves as evidence of participation in the discussion. It does not necessarily mean that the employee agrees with the rating.

+ Discuss and/or deal with performance problems at the time that they occurred. Management's motive in a poor performance discharge may be questioned if the incident prompting discharge occurred substantially prior to the time of discharge.

+ Do not avoid poor performance ratings for fear of discrimination charges. Rather, address performance issues consistently for all employees on a timely basis.

+ Speak with your superior or the human resource specialist if unsure about dealing with performance problems or consistency in performance ratings.

+ Clearly specify a final warning on the performance appraisal if performance is so poor that discharge may occur.

+ Avoid contrived or backdated appraisals. Avoid unreasonably harsh treatment of the employee to cause resignation.

+ Be consistent with performance ratings or feedback and any corresponding pay adjustments. If poor performance is evident, document it as a basis to delay or deny a pay adjustment. Inconsistency will reflect poorly in any subsequent legal proceedings.

+ Avoid making any discriminatory notes on performance management records or in any made statements during performance discussions.

Summary

Performance management, like all other employment decisions, is subject to state and federal labor laws and regulations. Administer performance management ratings fairly to avoid discrimination. Accurate ratings are important because performance appraisals can become evidence in legal proceedings. Having documentation of issues relating to poor performance or other adverse employment actions can support management's action in the event of a legal claim. Avoid using the performance management process in an unreasonably harsh manner that could be judged as constructive discharge.

Improving Your Performance Management Process

Room for Improvement

Every team leader or supervisor who has conducted performance discussions has probably felt that the evaluation process could be improved. Likewise, human resource specialists sometimes assert that managers and supervisors could do a better job of conducting performance discussions. To assist team leaders or supervisors in providing better performance evaluations and more productive discussions, this section identifies common problems and offers suggestions for improvement.

Typical Appraisal Errors and Solutions

There are a number of typical errors made by team leaders or supervisors when preparing a performance evaluation. These are highlighted below:

Inadequate Preparation - In the press of daily business activities, a team leader or supervisor may feel that he or she doesn't have a lot of time to spend on performance evaluations with each employee. Consequently, the supervisor quickly fills out the performance rating form with very little preparation or thought. As a result, the appraisal is likely to be incomplete, inaccurate, and lacking in detail.

Solution: Plan ahead for performance discussions. Maintain performance notes or records. Set aside time to prepare evaluations properly.

Halo Effect - The "halo effect" error is a tendency to generalize overall performance based on a single characteristic. For example, a worker may be highly articulate and friendly but with inadequate work skills and productivity. If the supervisor gives overall high ratings to this friendly employee, a "halo effect" error has occurred.

Solution: team leaders and supervisors need to be aware of this tendency and make a conscious effort to avoid it. Greater use of objective work data compared to standards or objectives helps to minimize the subjectivity of general impressions.

Strict or Easy Ratings - Some team leaders and supervisors tend to be strict raters while others are more lenient and generous with high ratings. Performance ratings tend to be inconsistent and unfair as a result of this type of error. This is caused by differing interpretations of policy or guidelines. If this practice continues unabated, employees view strict ratings as unfair. Ultimately, the credibility and objectivity of the evaluation process may be questioned by employees or supervisors alike.

Solution: Define workplace policies and clarify performance standards to achieve a better consensus among supervisors. Define and use performance rating definitions. Participate in team performance ratings where several team leaders or supervisors rate employee performance. Arrange to have performance evaluations reviewed by a higher-level manager and/or a human resource specialist who can catch inconsistencies in performance ratings. Conduct training for supervisors to promote better understanding and consistency in ratings.

Average Ratings - In the rush to quickly prepare performance evaluations, a team leader or supervisor may mark all employees with average ratings. Other raters, reluctant to confront an employee's performance problem, may make average ratings when a lower or poor performance rating should have been given. In both situations, the team leader or supervisor's action fails to advise the employee of poor performance and tends to perpetuate the performance problem. In cases of poor performance resulting in subsequent discharge, this failure to accurately record performance ratings will create a liability for the employer.

Solution: Plan and allow sufficient time to properly prepare performance appraisals. Key performance ratings to goals, work standards, or other work data. Let the objectivity of the data help to justify high, low, or average ratings. Arrange to have performance appraisals reviewed by a second-level manager who is likely to be aware of performance deficiencies.

Inflated or Above Average Ratings - In performance

evaluations at many companies, there is a tendency for team leaders or supervisors to inflate performance ratings. This tendency causes an overwhelming majority of employees to be rated in an "above average" performance category. Inflated ratings typically occur because supervisors want to be a "nice guy" and tell employees what they want to hear, "that your work is better than average." (After all, who wants to be told that you are just average?) Further, above-average ratings mean that the team leader or supervisor can recommend a better than average pay increase, thus perpetuating that nice guy role. Inflated ratings also tend to occur when rating a long-term employee. The main problem with inflated ratings is an unrealistic employee perception. Sooner or later another team leader or supervisor will accurately rate this employee lower, causing morale problems.

Solution: Avoid the subjectivity of this problem by defining primary job responsibilities and performance goals or expectations. Train raters on the proper interpretation of performance criteria. Consider separate pay and performance discussions. The human resource manager or a higher-level manager can review evaluations and require supervisors to justify "above average" ratings with performance data.

Recency Error - Our recollection of recent events is fresher and clearer than the memory of events occurring six to 12 months ago. As a result, there is an easy tendency for a supervisor to base performance ratings on work activities occurring in the last month. The performance evaluation, however, should reflect the full rating period, whether the rating period is monthly or quarterly or annually.

Solution: Be sure to provide daily performance feedback. Don't wait until the end of the rating period to recall performance issues. Keep a file of work samples, reports, or information which reflects performance results during the whole rating period and prepare the evaluation based upon this information.

Late Ratings - When the team leader or supervisor misses the normal schedule for an appraisal, the employee becomes concerned about performance and pay issues. Typical excuses for late appraisals offered by supervisors are very hectic schedules, a large number of employees, or business travel conflicts. However, timely conduct of performance checks or periodic evaluations is essential in maintaining the credibility of an effective performance management process.

Solution: Know the policy or practice at your firm and plan your schedule to complete performance discussions on time. Use your calendar app on your phone or computer system to notify yourself and the respective employee of planned performance discussions. In the event, you encounter a conflicting priority, re-schedule a new date, and stick to it.

Personal Prejudices - A team leader's or supervisor's personal prejudices or bias can adversely influence an employee's performance ratings. A bias against an employee due to age, race, sex, or other protected category is a clear violation of equal employment opportunity laws. Bias also may be based on other factors not defined in labor laws, such as personality conflicts, smokers versus non-smokers, or other similar issues. If the team leader or supervisor fails to recognize the prejudice, it can affect performance ratings, employee attitudes, and even result in legal claims against the company.

Solution: recognizing one's biases and prejudices is the first step in attempting to change. Defining objective performance criteria helps to minimize reliance on subjective factors. Performance appraisals conducted by multiple raters are another approach to minimize bias. Review of performance evaluations by higher-level managers or a human resource specialist provides a check against bias or prejudice. Train team leaders or supervisors to recognize and deal with biases.

Revitalizing a Stale Performance Management Program

After a few years of performance evaluations, some supervisors allow the appraisal process to become stale. Team leaders or supervisors claim that, after years of performance discussions, there is nothing new to be said. In reality, however, this situation is a reflection of the supervisor's attitude which is becoming stale - probably due to laziness or lack of initiative.

Every organization experiences change. New customers with new orders, different products, changing technologies, computerization, automation, competitive pressures, controlling costs or improving efficiencies are common examples of change occurring in the workplace. These changes require planning, implementing, training, and evaluating results.

110

A team leader or supervisor who is involved in workplace change or who exercises initiative to improve work activities will not become stale. And, performance discussions conducted by that team leader or supervisor will not become stale. Several key suggestions are offered to prevent the performance management process from becoming stale.

+ Honestly assess your performance evaluation techniques. (Use the self-audit checklist which follows.) If you have allowed the process to become stale, you are not challenging yourself or your employees to continually improve.

+ Define performance improvement goals for yourself, your department, and your employees. Aim for better quality, friendlier service, and more efficient completion of tasks. Honestly rate the results.

+ Introduce a new element into the performance management process. Several examples are offered: Have employees do a self-rating for comparison with your rating. Ask employees to rate your performance. Elicit input from other team leaders or supervisors for a team rating process. Separate performance and pay discussions if these are normally conducted simultaneously. Confer with superiors or human resources specialists as appropriate when seeking to introduce new processes or procedures into the performance management process.

Illustrative Case Example
"Controlling Inflation"

An office products company had a performance management process in place for several years. After a while, management noted an excessive number of very high-performance ratings, in spite of some serious productivity problems in various departments. Investigation revealed that numerous supervisors were inflating performance ratings to get higher pay increases for employees. Management took the following steps to correct the situation:

- Performance ratings were re-examined for inconsistencies compared to productivity problems. Supervisors and managers met to identify accurate ratings based on actual results.

- Managers defined objective performance goals for each department, focusing on timeliness of work completion, reduction of errors, and control of costs.

- Monthly performance briefings were instituted to provide feedback to employees comparing results achieved to the performance goals and measures.

- The human resource specialist developed performance rating definitions with examples to aid supervisors in distinguishing between poor, good, or superior performance ratings.

- Supervisors were trained in providing positive performance discussions and feedback techniques, as well as dealing with employee performance problems.

***

Summary

In most performance management processes, there is room for improvement. Common performance evaluation errors include inadequate planning or preparation, inaccurate or subjective ratings, biases, or failure to follow rating guidelines. A self-audit is provided to aid supervisors and managers in improving their performance appraisal techniques. Among the techniques to improve performance appraisals are the following: Plan for evaluations, maintain performance notes, and compare performance to objective work data. Follow policies and procedures. Use performance rating definitions. Arrange to have evaluations reviewed by a superior or human resources specialist. Continually challenge yourself and your department with performance improvement goals to keep performance evaluations from becoming stale.

Appendix

Self-Audit Your Performance Management
Sample Performance Evaluation Policy
Performance Rating Definitions
Example of Terms for Performance Levels
Pay for Performance Strategies
Anticipate Typical Employee Questions

Self-Audit Your Performance Management
A Checklist for Team Leaders, Supervisors and Managers

Use this self-audit to check your effectiveness in conducting effective performance appraisals.

1. Do you provide performance feedback to employees on a day to day or periodic basis? **Yes No**

2. Do you have a current and accurate job description or list of responsibilities for each employee under your supervision? **Yes No**

3. Have you defined and communicated performance expectations, goals, or standards for your employees? **Yes No**

4. Do you maintain any productivity or performance-related records for your work unit which can be used to help appraise performance? **Yes No**

5. Do you document poor performance on a performance evaluation or disciplinary warning in your performance management system? **Yes No**

6. Do you prepare performance evaluations on time in accordance with the policy or practice of your organization? **Yes No**

7. Do you refer to work samples or relevant job records when preparing a performance evaluation in order to provide an accurate and detailed assessment of the employee's performance? **Yes No**

8. Do you advise the employee in advance when scheduling a performance discussion? **Yes No**

9. Do you discuss unusual or troublesome employee performance issues with your superior or human resource specialist? **Yes No**

10. Do you conduct performance discussions in an office or area which assures privacy? **Yes No**

11. Do you discuss an employee's work performance on an objective and constructive basis which avoids personal insults or unreasonable criticism? **Yes No**

12. Do you give the employee credit for achievements and recognize accomplishments? **Yes No**

13. Do you offer constructive suggestions for improvement of

performance when needed? **Yes No**

14. Do you review relevant policies, guidelines, or performance definitions in order to provide consistent ratings? **Yes No**

15. Have you obtained any required approvals from superiors or the human resource specialist prior to discussing performance or pay issues? **Yes No**

16. Do you encourage employee comments and questions during the performance appraisal discussion? **Yes No**

17. Do you make written comments about specific performance issues on the evaluation document to clarify or explain performance ratings? **Yes No**

18. Do you obtain the employee's signature on the performance evaluation document? **Yes No**

19. Do you document specific performance deficiencies on the performance discussion and communicate a final warning in situations where discharge may be likely? **Yes No**

20. Have you followed the procedures for performance evaluation, discipline, or discharge in your firm's management policy, employee handbook, or union agreement? **Yes No**

Check your results - Score five points for each Yes answer. Total your score and rate your performance appraisal practices according to the following scale:

100 - 85 You are using sound performance management practices.

80 - 65 You need to improve performance management practices.

60 or below Your performance evaluation practices may cause serious employee relations problems or legal liability. Immediate improvement is needed.

Sample Performance Evaluation Policy

The following sample performance evaluation policy is compiled from policies at various organizations. It includes all the elements that a basic performance management process should contain. This sample may be adapted to meet the needs of your organization. The specific wording of any policy should be chosen to meet the particular circumstances of the company implementing the policy.

Performance Evaluation Policy

I. PURPOSE

To define the policy of the company to assure that employees receive periodic performance feedback, recognition, and corrective instructions to promote effective job performance.

II. COVERAGE

All employees.

III. MANAGEMENT RESPONSIBILITIES

A. Each team leader, supervisor or manager is responsible for guiding team members to achieve their maximum potential and to aid their contribution to the goals of the company. To promote consistency and objectivity, each performance evaluation shall be reviewed by the next higher-level manager and the Manager of Human Resources.

B. All performance management process should be conducted in an objective manner which avoids discrimination on the basis of race, color, religion, sex, national origin, age, physical or mental disability, status as a military reservist or veteran, or any other protected class defined by state or local law.

C. Employees are expected to perform essential job functions on a timely basis interacting with peers or customers or others on a respectful and professional basis, in compliance with company policies. A reasonable accommodation may be made for qualified individuals because of disability, or pregnancy or religion.

IV. POLICY GUIDELINES

A. Procedure

1. Each team leader, supervisor or manager is responsible for

conducting an informal performance feedback discussion each calendar quarter. The feedback may identify or clarify priorities, note interim achievement towards any specified goals, review of performance data, along with feedback on performance behavior and cooperation with team members.

2. Each team leader, supervisor or manager is responsible for conducting a performance re-cap after four quarters, and for defining new performance goal definitions to re-align with annual corporate goals. Quantified performance measures may be defined as appropriate along with suitable interim benchmarks. Career interests shall be explored and definition of training or job task assignments may be specified to aid in further career development.

3. The team leader, supervisor or manager is accountable to address and correct performance problems at any time deemed necessary. Performance data or documentation may be identified to support this discussion. If deemed necessary, a Performance Improvement Plan may be implemented for the coming quarter. The preparer should consult with superior management and/or human resources when developing a performance improvement plan.

4. The company uses a "Performance-check" software system as its designated performance management system. "Performance-check" systems are used to document performance check discussions, performance goals, achievement results, and performance improvement plans. The Human Resources manager is the System administrator for the "Performance-check" software system.

5. The team leader, supervisor or manager should refer to the "Performance-check" software system for policy guidelines, performance rating definitions, employee objectives, samples of individual productivity records, and related data when conducting performance management discussions. The system provides fill in the blank models to guide the performance feedback and goal-setting discussions.

7. The manager may require that team leaders and supervisors review the pending performance checks with the manager prior to discussion with the employee.

8. "Performance-check" system permits E-signature by the

rater and the employee. The employee may submit written comments relating to the rating. Likewise, the rater may make written comments in the space provided to clarify or explain ratings.

9. In the event that the individual's performance warrants a pay adjustment recommendation, see company policy on pay administration.

10. The completed fourth-quarter performance re-cap is reviewed by the superior manager(s) and human resources.

11. The performance feedback discussions should be conducted in a private room or office. Approximately a 30 - 45-minute discussion is recommended.

12. At the conclusion of the performance feedback discussion, the performance check record is retained by Human Resources in the Human Resources Information System. The employee has access to view his-her own records in the system.

Performance Rating Definitions

Many performance evaluation systems rate performance using some form of numerical scale or descriptive rating level. Difficulties in obtaining consistency in ratings among supervisors often stem from inadequate guidelines for defining the various performance rating levels. Nearly half of employers responding to the Mercer 2018/2019 US Compensation Planning Survey reported using five levels of performance ratings in performance evaluation processes. The different performance rating levels help to distinguish levels of employee job performance from outstanding performance down to poor performance.[40] To assist in distinguishing between various levels of performance, performance rating definitions are provided on the pages that follow:

Encourage team leaders or supervisors to use the performance rating definitions to achieve greater consistency of performance ratings among the various raters.

Performance Rating Guidelines

The care and accuracy with which each performance evaluation is made will affect its overall benefit to the employee and the Company. In order to help assure fair and uniform ratings, the following general rating definitions are provided:

Performance level # 1 - Unsatisfactory work is characterized by one or more of the following actions:

Frequent difficulties in accomplishing simple or routine tasks, excessive or obvious errors which may not be easily corrected, unnecessary waste of time or damage to product or equipment, frequent absences or tardies, or disregard for instructions. Unacceptable performance normally requires very close supervision. Failure to improve is grounds for dismissal.

Common examples of unsatisfactory performance include one or more of the following:
- Failure or refusal to perform assigned tasks.
- Failure or refusal to perform reasonable tasks in response to customer requests or management direction.
- Disregard for instructions from superior.
- Inability to complete simple assignments.
- Failing to observe work procedures.
- Negligent handling or use of equipment or products.
- Making repeated errors, or mistakes.
- Conveying a belligerent, angry, threatening, or intimidating attitude to customers or fellow employees.
- Frequently missing work.
- Frequently reporting to work late or returning late from lunch.
- Failing to recognize and correct obvious errors.

Performance level # 2 - Marginal work is characterized by one or more of the following actions: Does bare minimum level of work to "get by," able to complete simple tasks but should be performing more routine or complex tasks considering experience or time on the job, may have frequent or minor errors which could be prevented or corrected by extra effort, attendance may be borderline and occasionally exceed normally allowable absences, or may take longer than normal to complete assigned tasks. Marginal performance normally requires moderate to frequent checking and supervision. Failure to improve could result in warnings which may lead to dismissal. A marginal performance rating may be appropriate for a new employee who is learning skills on the job.

Common examples of marginal performance include one or more of the following:

- Occasional or periodic failure to perform assigned tasks.
- Occasional or periodic failure to perform reasonable tasks in response to customer requests.
- Experiences some difficulty in accomplishing routine work assignments.
- Takes longer than normal to complete routine tasks.
- Makes errors or mistakes even after corrective instruction.
- Fails to check own work to catch and correct errors.
- May occasionally display an angry, unpleasant, or inappropriate attitude to customers or fellow employees.
- Performs work in a "borderline" fashion.
- Lateness or absences border on being excessive.
- A supervisor or another employee may need to check the employee's work on a frequent basis.

Performance level # 3 - Good work is a reasonable and acceptable performance level for most employees. Good work is characterized by the following actions: Regular attendance with only a few absences or tardies, completion of routine work tasks on time, and meeting quality norms with a minimum amount of errors. Good performance normally requires general supervision and occasional checking to assist the employee to resolve complex job problems.

Common examples of good work include one or more of the following:

- Good performance is acceptable and normal for most employees.
- Routine assignments or tasks are completed on time.
- Work is performed accurately with only a few errors which are usually caught and corrected by the employee.
- Attendance is regular and dependable with only an occasional absence or tardiness occurring.
- May need some assistance or checking on complex work or new assignments, but shows an effort to complete tasks on own.
- Normally available to work extra hours as assigned.
- Accepts new tasks or assignments without resistance.
- Only occasional checking or instructions by the supervisor are

needed.
- Normally portrays a pleasant attitude and appearance appropriate for the job.

Performance level # 4 - Superior work performance is performance that is above average, exceeding basic and acceptable performance norms or standards. Superior work is characterized by the following actions: Reliable on-time attendance with very few instances of absence well under permissible norms for absences or lateness, dependable completion of routine and most complex work tasks on time or occasionally ahead of schedule, with demonstrated proficiency to meet or exceed quality norms on most jobs. A superior worker can be depended upon to work cooperatively and complete tasks with a minimum of supervision.

Common examples of superior performance include one or more of the following:

- Performance productivity generally exceeds performance norms or standards.
- Superior work is clearly above average with better results than many employees.
- Routine tasks are completed accurately and usually ahead of schedule.
- Capably handles complex or unusual tasks or assignments with only minimal direction from superior.
- Demonstrates reliable and dependable attendance with only a rare instance of absence or lateness.
- Willingly accepts extra tasks, assignments, or overtime work.
- The quality or accuracy of work is very high, errors are rare.
- Demonstrates diligence to catch and correct errors of self and others.
- Consistently portrays a pleasant, professional attitude and appearance, even under pressure or trying circumstances.
- Recognizes and prevents errors, offers solutions to problems, suggests improvements in products or services.

Performance level # 5 - Outstanding work performance is

performance that consistently produces outstanding results clearly exceeding the performance levels and quality norms of a large majority of other employees. Outstanding work is characterized by the speedy, efficient, and accurate accomplishment of tasks in a cooperative manner plus demonstrated initiative to solve complex problems and assist fellow employees. An excellent employee can be relied upon to organize and complete complex tasks on time or frequently ahead of schedule with a minimum of supervision.

Common examples of outstanding performance include one or more of the following:

+ Performance productivity consistently exceeds performance norms or standards.
+ Outstanding work clearly exceeds levels of nearly all other employees, resulting from efforts that are "above and beyond the call of duty."
+ Exercises initiative to plan and coordinate complex tasks or assignments.
+ Completes own tasks accurately and consistently ahead of schedule and assists others to complete tasks or resolve difficulties.
+ Demonstrates a high level of reliability, dependability with near-perfect attendance.
+ Quality and accuracy are near perfect.
+ Suggests and implements procedures to improve quality or reduce errors.
+ Demonstrates leadership ability to exercise control of emergency or pressure situations and prompting others to maintain a pleasant professional attitude.

Examples of terms for performance levels

Various terms have been used by firms to describe or distinguish levels of performance. Firms often select the terms to correlate with the culture of the business and the firm's employee relations philosophies. Samples are shown with five and with three performance level distinctions. Numerical scores are sometimes used to correlate to the performance level, generally with one (1) being low and five (5) being high-performance level. Samples were drawn from the public domain.

Unsatisfactory Performance
Marginal Performance
Good Performance
Superior Performance
Outstanding Performance

Leading Performance
Strong Performance
Solid Performance
Building Performance
Not meeting expectations

Exceptional Performance
Exceeds Expectations
Fully Meets Expectations
Needs Improvement
Unsatisfactory Performance

Did not meet key objectives
Met some key objectives
Met key objectives
Exceeded most key objectives
Significantly exceeded key objectives

Sample of three-level performance terms
Needs Improvement
Successful
Exceptional

Pay for Performance Strategies

Some firms provide instructional guidelines to aid team leaders or supervisors in making pay adjustments. Such strategies may consider performance rating, size of pay adjustment, timing of pay adjustment, or the employee's pay rate position within the salary range for the job. Examples are summarized below.

Performance rating affects size pay adjustment: the size of the pay adjustment may be correlated to the performance rating, such as (1) unacceptable work receives a 0% pay adjustment, satisfactory work receives a 3% pay adjustment, and superior work receives a 6% pay adjustment.

Performance rating affects timing of pay adjustment: the frequency or timing of the pay adjustment may be accelerated or delayed depending on the employees job performance, such as (1) unacceptable performance justifies delaying or denying a pay adjustment, (2) satisfactory performance may receive pay adjustment on normal 12 month interval, and (3) superior performance is rewarded with an accelerated pay increase schedule after 6 or 9 months.

Position in pay range also may be considered, providing greater flexibility in the size of pay adjustment or timing of pay adjustment for individuals who are paid below the midpoint of the pay range, and pay adjustments may be lower or delayed for individuals who are above the maximum rate for the pay range.

Anticipate Employee Comments & Questions
How do you handle the employee who says . . . . ?

1. "Don't tell me about being late! I know that Maria and Marsha were late more than me!"
   Your reply:

_____

2. "OK, let's get this over with. What kind of raise do I get?"
   Your reply:

_____

3. "That's not a fair rating. I know for a fact that Software Development employees missed more deadlines and they were rated Excellent."
   Your reply:

_____

4. "You're always picking on me. I could do my job better if you left me alone!"
   Your reply:

_____

5. "It's not my fault. We always get bad order specs from Sales. I just enter the orders."
   Your reply:

_____

6. "How can you say that? I've always had good reviews!"
   Your Reply:

_____

126

Answering Employee Questions

1. When do I get a review?

2. When are performance evaluations given?

3. These performance goals are too hard to reach. Where do they come from?

4. Why are you giving me a goal for customer returns? That is beyond my control.

5. Will I get a pay raise every 6 months?

6. How will the evaluation affect my pay?

7. What if I disagree with my performance rating?

8. How can you blame me? The rest of the team should be rated the same."

9. Why should I sign this review? I don't think it is fair.

Endnotes:

[1] Hockly, Nicky, "The digital generation," ELT Journal, 65(3):322-325. June 2011.

[2] 2017 Inventory of Total Rewards & Practices, World at Work Survey conducted by World at Work, P. 20. https://www.worldatwork.org/docs/research-and-surveys/Report_FINAL1.pdf.

[3] IBID.P. 134.

[4] Waters, Shonna, "Should Organizations Pay for Performance?" SHRM White Paper, Oct. 27, 2017.

[5] 2017 Inventory of Total Rewards & Practices, 134.

[6] 6 Hearn, Stuart, "5 Game Changing Performance Management Trends for 2018. Blog of 05 Dec 2017. https://www.clearreview.com/5-performance-management-trends-2018/

[7] 7 By Staff author; "Survey: US Employers Rethinking Compensation Programs," Gartner Talent Daily, 6-25-18, cebglobal.com

[8] Deloitte 2019 Human Capital Trends; Bersen, Josh; Denny, Brad; Durme, Yves Van; Hauptman, Maren; Indranil, Roy; Schwartz, Jeff; and Volini, Errica; Delloitte "2019 Human Capital Trends Leading the social enterprise – Reinvent with a human focus". P2 https://www2.deloitte.com/content/dam/insights/us/articles/5136_HC-Trends-2019/DI_HC-Trends-2019.pdf

[9] IBID.P5.

[10] Cunningham, Lillian, "In big move, Accenture will get rid of annual performance review and rankings," Washington Post, July 21, 2015.

[11] ETS Blog, "Replacing performance ratings…How Amazon, Deloitte and Google do it," ETS Consultancy & HR Technology, https://www.etsplc.com/blog/replacing-performance-ratings-how-amazon-deloitte-and-google-do-it/.

[12] Gurchiek, Kathy, "How to Make Ratingless Performance Management Systems Work," 6-19-2017SHRM White Paper Article," www.shrm.org.

[13] Mizne, David, "7 Unexpected Employee Performance Management Trends to Watch for in 2019," 15Five Blog, https://www.15five.com/blog/employee-performance-management-trends-2019/

[14] Hearn, Stuart.

[15] Heathfield, Susan, "5 Tips for Managing Millennials," The Balance Careers, 2-11-2019, www.thebalancecareers.com.

[16] Stein, Guido, "Nine tips for Managing Millenials," Forbes, IESE Business School contributor, 9-8-2016, www.forbes.com/sites/iese/2016/09/08/managing-millennials-nine-tips/#44e900b2cd8a.

[17] . Hicks, Maureen Soyars, "Flexible jobs give workers choices," Monthly Labor Review, May 2017, https://www.bls.gov/opub/mlr/2017/beyond-bls/flexible-jobs-give-workers-choices.htm

[18] The rise of crowdsourcing J Howe - Wired magazine, 6-6-06 vol 14, issue 6, pp 1-4, https://www.wired.com/2006/06/crowds/

[19] *Contingent and Alternative Employment Arrangements Summary, News Release, June 7, 2018, USDL-18-0942, https://www.bls.gov/news.release/conemp.nr0.htm*

[20] IBID.

[21] IBID.

[22] IBID.

[23] Deloitte 2019 Human Capital Trends, P. 26.

[24] Hubbartt, William S. "What You Ought to Know About Participating in Employee Committees and Work Teams, Commerce Clearing House, 1995, p. 11-19.

[25] 2017 World at Work, P. 26.

[26] 26 Dulebohn, James H., and Hoch, Julia E., "Virtual Teams in Organizations," Human Resource Management Review, 27 (2017) 569-574.

[27] Kirkman, Bradley L., Rosen, Benson, Gibson, Cristina B., Tesluk, Paul E., McPherson, Simon O., " Five challenges to virtual team success: Lessons from Sabre, Inc." Acadamy of Management Executive, 2002, Vol 16, No 3.

[28] Lipnack, Jessica, and Stamps, Jeffrey, "VirtualTeams: The New Way to Work," Strategy & Leadership, Jan/Feb, 1999; 27, 1, p. 14.

[29] Young, Lauren, "How to create connections at work in the age of isolation," Reuters, April 1, 2019, /www.reuters.com/article/us-world-work-remoteworkers/how-to-create-connections-at-work-in-the-age-of-isolation-idUSKCN1RO13J.

[30] Kohnke, Bas, "How to create a healthy feedback culture," HRZone, April 1, 2019. https://www.hrzone.com/talent/development/how-to-create-a-healthy-feedback-culture.

[31] Low, Tim, "Will They Stay or Will They Go? – The 2019 Compensation Best Practices Report. Pay Scale, P. 7.

[32] Mason, Lauren, and Sardone, Mary Ann, "2018/2019 United States Compensation Planning," Mercer LLC.

[33] 2017 World at Work, P 118.

[34] Mercer 2018/2019, P

[35] Low, Tim, Pay Scale 2019 Best Practices Report, P. 18.

[36] 2018 Deloitte Global Human Captial Trends, P. 33.

[37] Maier, Steffen, "7 New Top Trends Top Companies Use to Separate Performance from Compensation," Entrepreneur, Feb.14, 2017. https://www.entrepreneur.com/article/287650

[38] Falcone, Paul, "Employment-at-Will vs. the Discharge-for-Just-Cause Only Standard: A Critical Employment Law Distinction, SHRM White Paper, Sept 26, 2016. WWW.SHRM.org.

[39] "Handling Internal Discrimination Complaints About Performance Evaluations," Tips for Small Businesses, EEOC.gov.

[40] Mercer 2018/2019.P.10.

About the Author:

William S. Hubbartt MSIR, SPHR has over 30 years of experience in human resource management including positions in industry, corporate, education, government and consulting. Hubbartt holds a MS Degree in Industrial Relations from Loyola University of Chicago. He was awarded a lifetime accreditation as a Senior Professional in Human Resources (SPHR), from the Human Resource Certification Institute.

William S. Hubbartt is a former EEOC Federal Investigator who handled investigations and achieved resolutions of employment discrimination complaints. Previously, Mr. Hubbartt was President of Hubbartt & Associates for 25 years, providing human resources consulting services for 300+ firms in the Chicago area and nationally. He is a former community college Adjunct Instructor in Human Resources. Mr. Hubbartt has published over 75 articles in national publications. Hubbartt holds a M.S. degree in Industrial Relations from Loyola University of Chicago. Mr. Hubbartt is the author of fiction and non-fiction materials including; "Personnel Policy Handbook - How to Prepare a Manual that Works" (McGraw-Hill, 1993), "Performance Appraisal Manual for Managers and Supervisors," (Commerce Clearing House, 1992), "What Every Employee Ought to Know About Performance Appraisal," (CCH, 1994), and "What You Ought to Know About Participating in Employee Committees and Work Teams,"(CCH, 1995), and "The New Battle Over Workplace Privacy," (AMACOM, 1998), "The Medical Privacy Rule- A Guide for Employers and Health Care Providers," (Hubbartt, 2003) and "The HIPAA Privacy Sourcebook," (SHRM, 2003) and The HIPAA Security Rule- A Guide for Employers and Health Care Providers," (Hubbartt, 2004).

Fiction works authored by Hubbartt: Lawman's Justice, Heavy Handed Justice, Justice for Abraham (2019), Six Bullet Justice, Death on the Santa Fe Trail, and The Last Score (Outlaws Publishing, 2018) Short story fiction includes placements in Zimbell House No Trace Anthology (2018) and the Ghost Stories Anthology (2017), Storyteller Anthology Magazine, Mondays are Murder, Heater – Fiction Magazine and Wilderness House Literary Review.

Acknowledgments

Certain information contained in Achieving Performance Results was drawn in part from other work by author Hubbartt, including: "Performance Appraisal Manual for Managers and Supervisors," (Commerce Clearing House, 1992), and "Improving Performance Results," (Hubbartt, 2007).

 A project like writing and producing a book cannot be done alone. I wish to thank family and friends for their support, valuable ideas and suggestions, including: Gloria D. Kwasniewski, Don Hubbartt, Jen Hubbartt, Mike Hubbartt, Mieke Olswang, Joel Vestuto, and Alex (Kwazzy) Kwasniewski.

List photo credits:
Front Cover: Photo by rawpixel.com from Pexels.
Office work team: Photo by rawpixel.com from Pexels.
Millenial female: Photo by Christina Morillo from Pexels.com.
Female working remotely:Photo by Bruce Mars from Pexels.com.
Lady Justice & law books: Image by Jessica 45 from Pixabay.
Young Lady entering data: Photo by Modce Photos from Pexels.
Man and woman talking seriously: Photo by rawpixel.com from Pexels.
Two young women talking: Photo by Tirachard Kumtanon from Pexels. com
Supreme Court building: Photo by Claire Aderson from Unsplash.com